EVALUATING RESEARCH
METHODS IN PSYCHOLOGY

For Romy

EVALUATING RESEARCH METHODS IN PSYCHOLOGY

A CASE STUDY APPROACH

GEORGE DUNBAR

BPS Blackwell

BLACKWELL PUBLISHING
350 Main Street, Malden, MA 02148-5020, USA
9600 Garsington Road, Oxford OX4 2DQ, UK
550 Swanston Street, Carlton, Victoria 3053, Australia

First published 2005 by The British Psychological Society and Blackwell
Publishing Ltd

1   2005

Library of Congress Cataloging-in-Publication Data

Dunbar, George (George L.)
    Evaluating research methods in psychology : a case study approach /
George Dunbar.
        p. cm.
    Includes bibliographical references and index.
    ISBN-13: 978-1-4051-2074-6 (hard cover : alk. paper)
    ISBN-10: 1-4051-2074-6 (hard cover : alk. paper)
    ISBN-13: 978-1-4051-2075-3 (pbk. : alk. paper)
    ISBN-10: 1-4051-2075-4 (pbk. : alk. paper)
    1. Psychology – Research – Methodology.   2. Psychology – Research –
Case studies.   I. Title.

    BF76.5.D85 2005
    150'.72–dc22

                                                        2004029159

A catalogue record for this title is available from the British Library.

Set in 10.5/12.5pt Photina
by Graphicraft Ltd., Hong Kong
Printed and bound in the United Kingdom
by TJ International, Padstow, Cornwall

The publisher's policy is to use permanent paper from mills that operate a
sustainable forestry policy, and which has been manufactured from pulp
processed using acid-free and elementary chlorine-free practices. Furthermore,
the publisher ensures that the text paper and cover board used have met
acceptable environmental accreditation standards.

For further information on
BPS Blackwell, visit our website:
www.bpsblackwell.co.uk

The British Psychological Society's free Research Digest e-mail service rounds
up the latest research and relates it to your syllabus in a user-friendly way.
To subscribe go to www.researchdigest.org.uk or send a blank e-mail to
subscribe-rd@lists.bps.org.uk

CONTENTS

CASE STUDIES

SOLUTIONS

PREFACE

This book illustrates and explains several important points and potential pitfalls in psychological research through a series of case studies. Each case describes a real piece of research, and asks you to consider whether the conclusions drawn are correct, or whether the results could be explained in some other way. The book is organized in much the same way as *Rival Hypotheses* (Huck & Sandler, published in the UK by HarperCollins, first published in 1979), which has, sadly, been out of print for some years.

Case studies are an excellent way to reinforce lecture material through independent study. Real case studies are interesting and engaging. The concreteness of detailed, realistic, examples helps you to understand the important issues involved, which can seem complex if presented in an abstract form, and helps you see the force of the difficulties that can arise. Evaluating the conclusions that can be drawn from a piece of evidence allows you to rehearse and develop critical thinking skills.

- You gain a deeper understanding of methodological problems;
- You gain an appreciation that sometimes it is hard to design research that is without any methodological limitation, for example in applied settings;
- You become better equipped to evaluate or review published research, knowing better what kinds of things to look for;
- You gain confidence in designing your own research, and develop some valuable competences to help you ask the right questions, and to self-evaluate your plans.

The book has four main sections. The first introduces some themes in psychological research methods. The second section contains the case studies, and the solutions follow in the third section. The fourth section recaps the core ideas that emerge through the case studies.

Each case study is kept as short and as concise as possible. Each explains the background to a study, the relevant aspects of the method, and sets out a conclusion that could be drawn from the original paper. Each time, I pose a question. The question asks you to consider whether the conclusion set out is valid, and, if not, to say why you think the results may have an alternative explanation. Inevitably, the summaries select aspects of the original research, and reflect my judgement about the relevant issues. In the same way, the solutions represent my own opinion. I aim to emphasize that the interpretation of research findings is up for debate, and that the field progresses through a process of discussion, further research, and the progressive refinement of explanations. If you are interested in particular pieces of research, I encourage you to go to the original articles, and to read them in full.

The book is best looked at as a set of resources, to be dipped into and used as needed. Although I have tried to order the case studies in a reasonable way, and I have placed some of the easier examples near the beginning, they do not follow one from another like chapters in a monograph. Very roughly, the first six cases form an introductory set. The cases then are broadly ordered in terms of the topic area of the original research. These topics include, in order, psychodynamically inspired research, psychopathology, memory and emotion (cases 7–16), educational and developmental psychology (cases 17–23), individual differences (including cases 4, 7, 18, 24–6), attention (cases 26, 27), psycholinguistics (cases 6, 28–30), interventions (cases 17, 22, 31–2, and 38), intelligence (cases 34–7), parapsychology (case 39), sports psychology (cases 41–2), and social psychology (cases 43–4). Some cases are really quite challenging. The more detailed and, in general, the more difficult cases are, the longer they tend to be. A table in the end of the book provides a cross-reference to help find relevant case studies connected to particular methodological issues. I have included several studies that illustrate ethical considerations, and these are also identified in the table. Many of the studies, and many of the most interesting pieces of research in general, span more than one basic topic.

I hope that the book will be useful to anyone studying research methods in psychology and to anyone who wants to critically evaluate published research. I hope that it will encourage you to participate actively in the process of psychological research, to debate findings, and to carry out new studies of your own.

I acknowledge the tremendous help and support I received from Will Maddox and Sarah Bird at Blackwell. D. Watson very kindly reviewed one of the cases that describes a piece of his own research. The book has also been improved considerably by the advice of two anonymous readers who reviewed the manuscript, and the comments of the referees of the original proposal. We have been concerned to be fair to the authors of the research described. Of course, I am responsible for errors that remain. Like all sciences, psychology is forged in the fire of criticism and refinement, and I hope that the original researchers will understand that the criticism is made with respect. The accompanying website (address on the back cover of the book) will provide space for authors to respond to the critiques presented in the following pages, and I invite them to contact me if they wish to do that.

1

EVIDENCE IN PSYCHOLOGY

In psychology, investigators try to understand human behavior and to explain the capacities that people have to see, feel, think, learn, communicate, and so on. Simply watching people and talking to them in an ordinary way does not lead us to a clear understanding. Our everyday observation is unsystematic and tells us little more than that people do think, communicate, and so on. Simply thinking about our own behavior or reflecting on our own inner mental lives is also not enough. Everyone from Freud to modern cognitive scientists agrees that there is more to it than the mind's eye can see. Worse, evidence from introspection often leads different people to different conclusions, and the method does not allow us to work out which conclusion is correct. Research methods are developed to allow investigators to draw conclusions about the phenomena that interest them, conclusions that others can have good grounds to accept.

This book is about the conclusions that are made from professional research studies. Examples are drawn from peer-reviewed journals and scholarly books. We are interested in the soundness of the methods used: Given the research method, can a particular conclusion be drawn? The style of reasoning is generally to try to find an alternative conclusion that could be drawn, a rival hypothesis. If we could explain the results in a different way, by drawing a different conclusion from the same evidence, then the original conclusion does not necessarily follow from the experiment. The aim is to explore the pitfalls of research in psychology. It is very difficult to conduct the perfect experiment in psychology, and we use case studies from professional research to illustrate some of the more common problems.

Research examples are taken from a range of areas of psychology, including cognitive, developmental, and social psychology. Here are some of the conclusions we'll be testing:

- playing video games leads to aggressive behavior;
- playing video games improves attention skills;
- children less than 1 year old can add and subtract;
- an intervention based on developing balance skills is an effective treatment for dyslexia;
- people with a thrill-seeking personality are more likely to have car accidents;
- if you drink alcohol, people of the opposite sex look prettier.

In some cases, the conclusions are plausible because they fit with our experience or our expectations. To many people, it is plausible that playing video games will lead to aggressive behavior because video games contain violent imagery, and engage players in simulated acts of violence. However, as scientists we need to test those expectations. It is not enough that some people think it is plausible. Others might argue that video games do not cause aggressive behavior because the violence is only simulated, and players easily separate fantasy from the real world. It is the role of research to provide evidence that lets us draw firm conclusions.

When you evaluate a piece of research, you are trying to decide just what conclusions can be drawn. The researcher will have written what they think follows from their study, but you have to make your own judgement. Often, you will not be convinced that the conclusion the researcher has drawn necessarily follows from their findings. It may be plausible, but there are other possible explanations. There are several aspects of a piece of research that you might criticize, and we now consider each in turn.

THE RESEARCH QUESTION

The first issue is whether the researchers have set out to answer a sensible question. Some research questions may not address an issue that you find interesting. Different people have different agendas, and different priorities. For example, some people approach topics in developmental psychology from the point of view of classroom practice, others have an interest in parenting, and still others are mainly interested in general theoretical questions about the influence of environment on development. Each of these perspectives highlights different issues. A study that aims to improve practice may not ask the type of question that a theoretician is primarily interested in. For instance, a classroom practitioner may want to know whether color illustrations make mathematics textbooks more effective. This may be an important practical question, but knowing the answer may be of limited importance for general theories of development.

Occasionally, a research project may pose a question in a way that is clearly too simplistic given existing knowledge. For example, a research project that asks whether some aspect of behavioral development is caused either by information encoded in DNA or by the environment is almost certainly asking too simplistic a question. Most aspects of development are clearly influenced both by genetic preparation and the environment together. The way that the genetic blueprint unfolds is influenced by the environment.

Another problem you may encounter is when a research project makes assumptions about the world that you do not accept. For example, several research programs have investigated psychological differences between races of people. However, many investigators would not accept that classifying people into races is scientifically meaningful. They would argue that the variation between people within a "race" is as great as variation between races, and they would point to the way that different cultures distinguish races in different ways. Bear in mind that the rejection of assumptions should be made on scientific grounds, rather than political ones. How much genetic and behavioral variation there is within "races" is an empirical issue that can be settled scientifically, and so is a legitimate basis for arguing against race as an important aspect of human classification.

A related criticism is that, even if the research question were answered, it would not get us anywhere to know the answer. This is a criticism made most often of studies of racial differences. A critic would argue that even if we do discover that one race is on average less intelligent than another it could not possibly make any practical difference: What conceivable change to public policy could be justified by such knowledge? Of course, that is a question about the politics of research. That is, what are the implications for choices we make as a society?

Studies can also be criticized for attempting to answer questions that the discipline is not in a position to answer effectively. Some questions just cannot be answered by scientific methods. For example, how much longer would World War II have continued if the US military had not dropped atomic weapons on two Japanese cities? There is no way to know. We cannot rerun the scenario with the same politicians in charge, playing it out alternately, with and without, atomic weapons. Another example with a slightly more psychological flavor is "would John Wayne have become a cowboy or a farmer if he had lived in the nineteenth century?." The best we can offer is an educated guess: Most probably, an actor.

The first thing to evaluate, then, is the research question. Is it answerable? Are its assumptions scientifically acceptable? Does it ask something interesting? One thing to bear in mind is that studies that have different objectives to your own can still be useful. For example, practical research on colored mathematics books could provide some information that a theorist would find useful if the **theory** made predictions that distinguished color and black and white images. For example, if you had a theory predicting that people make more use of top down information when interpreting black and white images, data on mathematics learning with black and white or color images could provide some interesting clues. Even if a study does not directly address the questions that interest you most, it can still be valuable to you.

THE TYPE OF DESIGN

There are several types of research **design**. The distinctions between them are important because they directly limit the types of conclusion that can be drawn from the study. The strongest conclusion that we aim to draw is a causal conclusion. A causal conclusion says that some **outcome** is caused by something. For example, if I press a key on my keyboard, that causes the corresponding letter to appear on the computer screen. You can only draw causal conclusions validly from true experiments.

In an experiment, you manipulate the **conditions** in which behavior occurs, and you randomly assign participants to different conditions. Both of these things are crucial.

There are other important aspects to causality. It is important to be able to say something about why the **manipulation** causes the **outcome**. This involves being able to explain the mechanism that leads from the causal variable to the effect.

For example, I could use an experiment to show that my cat comes to the door of my house when I put my key in the lock. The claim that the sound causes the cat to come is made more convincing if

I can offer a causal mechanism to explain how the sound of the key affects my cat's behavior. This helps in two ways. First, we do not like mystery in science. If I make the claim that my cat comes to the door of my house when I step off the bus, a mile away, you will be sceptical because there is a mystery about how the cat could know that I will soon be home. It is reasonable to claim that the cat hears the sound of a key in the lock and responds to that, but it is not easy to understand how it could detect the sound of me stepping off the bus a mile away. The second way it helps is it gives us specific predictions that we can test. If the cat responds because it hears the key, we can test this by blocking her ears. The prediction is that she will not come when her ears are blocked, because the causal mechanism has been blocked.

Another way to support a causal claim is to show that the extent of a response varies in proportion to variation in the magnitude of the hypothesized cause. For example, if I hypothesize that it is the alcohol in wine that makes people react more slowly, showing that higher doses of alcohol cause greater amounts of slowing will support the causal conclusion.

A second important type of study **design** is called a **quasi-experiment**. In quasi-experiments, different levels of an **independent variable** are contrasted to see if they are associated with different outcomes, but participants are not randomly assigned to groups. Instead, they are tested in existing, ready-formed groups. Sometimes this is completely unavoidable. For example, studies which contrast male and female responses recruit participants who are already either male or female, and there really is no way round that. In other cases, it may be done for convenience. For example, a researcher who is comparing two teaching methods may run the first method with one class of children, and use a different class for the other method. It may just not be practical to mix up the two classes by **random assignment** only for the sake of the research study.

The difficulty with quasi-experiments is that you cannot be sure that the difference between the groups you are interested in is the only important difference between them. For example, the average age of one class might be a few months higher than the other. If they do better, it could be because they were older, not because the teaching method was better. The reason for **random assignment** in experiments is to try to even out all the other possible differences. If children were randomly assigned to the two teaching methods, then, in the long run, across many experiments, we would expect the two groups to have the same mean age. We would also expect them to be, on average, equal on every other conceivable variable.

Correlational designs look at the association between two variables. For example, we could look at the correlation between IQ scores and income. If we do that, we will usually find that people with higher IQ scores have higher yearly incomes. However, correlational designs do not permit causal conclusions. Just because there is a high correlation it does not mean that wealthy people are rich because they have high IQ scores. It could be that their wealth leads them to have high IQ scores. This could happen if rich people were able to afford better nourishment and better education. Alternatively, it could be some other variable. For example, perhaps poor people in our sample tend to live in different areas from the rich, where they are subject to environmental pollution. It could be a pollutant rather than anything directly connected to wealth that causes poorer cognitive development.

Correlational designs need not use **correlation statistics**, and it is important to be able to recognize correlational designs even when they use other statistical methods. For example, I could divide a sample of participants into three groups, based on IQ score: high, medium, and low. I could then do a one-way ANOVA to test whether the average income of the groups is different. Although this study does not use correlation statistics to test the hypothesis, it still has a correlational design. If the three groups do differ in terms of income, we still have no idea whether wealth affects IQ, IQ affects wealth, or something else.

If correlational designs only allow relatively weak conclusions to be drawn, why do people use them? Why doesn't everyone do experiments all the time? There are two answers to this. First, some researchers do choose to avoid correlational designs. They work in areas of psychology where hypotheses can be tested experimentally, and this allows them to draw relatively strong conclusions. However, many researchers use correlational designs because they are interested in questions that would be hard to address experimentally, either for practical or for ethical reasons. For instance, it is difficult to imagine being able to run an experiment where participants were randomly assigned to high or low income groups at birth to see whether income affects intelligence. Apart from the obvious ethical problem (how would you like your child to be assigned to the low income condition?), funding might be tricky.

A fourth type of study is the **observational study**. In an observational study, the researcher observes and records behavior in a natural environment. The advantage of an observational study is that the researcher gets to look at behavior that is expressed by the participants largely of their own volition. When experimenters set up tasks or situations in the laboratory, there is always a worry that the resulting behavior is quite specific to the experimental conditions. If the participants adapt their responses to the experiment, then their behavior may not be a good reflection of their behavior in other situations.

Observational studies can be useful in establishing that certain types of behavior do occur. For example, an observational study could demonstrate that infants do smile at their mothers from a certain age. They can also be useful for generating ideas in the early stages of a research programme. This is especially helpful when the researcher has little prior knowledge of the topic, or wants to set aside their expectations. For example, if you were interested in how expert surgeons assess a case, you could begin by observing surgeons at work. You could observe how often they make notes, who they talk to, what kinds of questions they ask. These observations could lead you to form hypotheses that can later be tested in formal experiments or quasi-experiments.

I have suggested that an advantage of observational research is that it allows the investigator to record behavior without interfering with the expression of that behavior, and without making any prior assumptions about how behaviors will occur. In practice, there are three ways in which observational research departs from this ideal model. First, researchers will almost always have some expectations about what the relevant types of behavior are. For example, I mentioned making notes and asking questions, but I did not mention the number of times the surgeon scratches him or herself. I implicitly assumed that scratching would not be important, but, of course, I could be wrong. Perhaps people scratch themselves more when they are unsure about a decision. If scratching is important, then my observations would have been incomplete. However, researchers have to make some selection of behaviors to record, if only for the practical reason that there is not time to record everything.

The second departure is that in observational research we will often set up situations for participants to experience. This allows us to compare the behavior of different participants more easily. For example, in a study I carried out with two colleagues, we observed participants crossing roads around the campus. However, we sent them all on the same route by asking them to go and buy some cookies at the campus shop. This gave us a more systematic set of observations than if we had simply observed people walking around a town, crossing roads on a route of their own choice.

A third departure is called **participant observation**. This is where the researcher participates in a situation and makes a record of the events and experiences that unfold. For example, a researcher who was interested in the behavior of sports fans might mix with the fans of a football team, but instead of declaring that he or she was a psychologist, would try to pass as a fellow supporter. In this case, the researcher is active in the situation, and clearly it is possible that they themselves could have a large influence on the behaviors that occur. Nevertheless, the researcher may feel that if subjects knew they were being observed in a psychological investigation, then that would create greater distortions in their behavior.

An important distinction to make is between exploratory studies and studies that test a **hypothesis**. Ideally, we use a theory to generate a hypothesis, and set up a study to test that hypothesis. For example, we have a theory about why my cat comes to the door when I turn my key in the lock. From that theory, we can generate the hypothesis that if the cat were made deaf it would not come. We could then set up an experiment to test this hypothesis. However, often our existing knowledge is not sufficiently well developed to do this. We may not be certain what the important variables that influence outcomes are, or we may not be sure how best to measure those variables. **Exploratory research** gathers data systematically to help us develop and refine our understanding. Eventually, we hope to reach the point when we can generate hypotheses to test.

The very best research programmes often combine different types of design. In early stages, they might use correlational or quasi-experimental designs to establish that certain relationships are likely, and then move to experimental designs in the later stages, once the relevant variables and clear hypotheses have been identified. An example from medicine was research that related smoking to disease. Early research showed that people who smoked were more likely to suffer certain serious illnesses. Nevertheless, some people argued that those correlational studies could not establish a causal relationship. What was needed was a set of experimental trials in which subjects were randomly assigned to smoke or not. Of course, it was not possible to use human participants, and the research used animals. In its early stages, researchers used designs that were appropriate and practical to take understanding forward.

In the later stages, experimental research was used to draw firm causal conclusions.

RELIABILITY AND VALIDITY

The value of a piece of research depends on its **reliability** and **validity**. Reliability concerns the consistency of measurements. Highly reliable measures will give the same scores from one occasion to the next. The reliability of questionnaires is usually calculated, and reported numerically. There are two common ways of doing this. First, researchers can check whether the same test produces consistent scores on separate occasions. For instance, the test might be given to a group of people this Monday, and again next Monday. A high correlation between the two sets of scores would indicate high **test–retest reliability**. A variation on this is to present **alternate forms**, also called **parallel** forms, of the test at different times. Alternate forms use similar but not identical items to measure the same **construct**. The advantage is that this should reduce the likelihood that practice with the test first time around will tend on its own to produce similar results on the later occasion.

The second common way to evaluate reliability is to evaluate a test against itself, to calculate the **internal consistency** of the test. Many questionnaires use a number of questions, all trying to get at the same underlying psychological construct. For example, a test of extroversion might have one item asking how often you go to parties, another asking whether you start conversations with strangers, and so on. If the test is reliable, responses to the questions should all tend to agree, they should all point in the same direction. If the test is reliable, people who say they like parties should tend to be the people who start conversations. Tests of internal consistency, such as the split-half test, or coefficient alpha, are most often quoted by researchers. When researchers develop new tests, they try out different items, and select the items that produce the greatest internal consistency.

Validity is what this book is mainly about. Valid measures convey information about the properties that you want to know about. For example, a measure of extroversion is valid if it really does measure extroversion. This type of validity is known as **construct validity**. It is possible for a test to accidentally measure something other than what the researcher intended. For instance, if I tried to measure extroversion by asking people whether they drove a sports car or a compact saloon, the responses might really be giving me information about wealth rather than extroversion.

All aspects of a piece of research can affect the **validity** of conclusions drawn from that study. For example, if the participants or materials are poorly selected, or if the design confounds variables, it may adversely affect the conclusions that can be drawn. The phrase internal validity is used to describe the overall connection between the variables the researcher has measured and the conclusions she wants to draw. A study has high internal validity when that connection is secure. Internal validity is compromised when the connection is weak. For example, if I compare groups with high and low levels of extroversion to see who smokes more, **internal validity** would be compromised by using unreliable or invalid measures of extroversion or smoking, or if extroversion was confounded with another variable, such as time of testing, age, wealth, or anything else. Anything that weakens inferences about the psychological **constructs** we are really interested in, reduces internal validity.

In research, we carry out testing in a specific situation, with a specific group of people. It is always legitimate to ask, would you get the same results in a different situation, or with different people? For example, if I study the emotional responses of women to video images, can I generalize the results to men? Or women in another culture? **External validity** is concerned with the **generalizability** of results to other situations and to other kinds of people, particularly the real world situations in which the researcher is most interested. For example, researchers studying road safety are especially concerned that findings they make in the laboratory would generalize to the road environment. A closely related concept is **ecological validity**, the question of whether the behavior studied corresponds to behavior that would occur in the real world. For example, if I study reading processes in the laboratory by presenting single words on a screen, how do I know whether the processes and strategies I observe in the laboratory are the same ones used in ordinary reading? It could be that participants use or even develop special strategies to cope with the experimental situation.

You will perhaps see that there is a trade-off between **internal** and **external validity**. The greatest control and precision is possible in the laboratory, where variables can be isolated, and manipulated or controlled, where materials can be selected carefully, and presented with precise timing. This helps secure high levels of internal validity.

However, there is the risk that laboratory research creates special environments, sufficiently detached from everyday situations that participants resort to special cognitive and behavioral strategies. Conversely, field research may be so contaminated by confounds and biases that no meaningful conclusion can be drawn.

THE SAMPLE

Psychological research uses human **participants**, and these have to be recruited somehow. There are three basic issues. First, there is the number of participants. Studies with a low number of participants may have too little power, and may therefore be unable to detect effects that do exist. Also, studies with fewer participants can examine fewer **independent variables**. Guidance on sample size can be found in good statistical textbooks, such as Tabachnik & Fidell (2001).

Second, there is the question of the incentive they are given. In many studies, participants are college students who participate because they have to, or volunteers who participate because they want to participate in research. Volunteers are likely to be more enthusiastic, cooperative, and eager to please. Subjects who have been pressed into participation may become bored and inattentive. When interpreting results, consider how these factors may affect the interpretation of the results. For example, volunteers may be more prone to **experimenter effects**, where they try to give the responses they think the experimenter wants them to give.

Third, samples are rarely a representative, **random**, sample of the entire **population**. Often, we use students: young, bright, frequently middle-class. If a **sample** is narrow, then it is important to be careful about generalizing the findings to other groups. For example, if a researcher does an experiment on color perception using only male students as participants, we should be cautious about accepting that the findings can be applied to women, because we know that there are forms of color blindness that only men can have. However, we probably would be willing to accept that the results generalize to other young men. To take a different example, if an investigator finds that female college students in the United States spend more money on make-up than textbooks, we would not conclude that the same was true of male professors in Germany, at least not without further evidence.

This can be a particular issue for standardized tests and questionnaires. Many tests provide a system to convert raw test scores into a standard score. For example, IQ tests convert raw test scores into IQ scores, which are designed to have a mean of 100 in the population as a whole. How do the test designers know which test score corresponds to the **population** mean? They run the test on a representative sample. The scores of the sample are used to define the norm. However, for many tests the sample used for norming is specific to a particular nation. Many tests are normed in the United States. If the test results are applied in a different **population**, then it is important to bear in mind that the norms may not be appropriate. For instance, someone may score low on a test for clinical depression not because they are clinically depressed, but because in their culture it is usual to respond to questions like those on the test in a particular way.

THE MATERIALS

In many experiments, participants are given items to consider. For example, they might be asked to look at pictures of everyday objects, read some sentences, or write down the meaning of a phrase. It is always worth having a careful look at the particular items chosen, because sometimes the choice of materials can bias the results.

For example, in many experiments on language, reading time is measured. For instance, an experimenter might test whether sentences are easier to read if they are in the form of a question or if they are in the form of a statement. It is important that the sentences are matched for word frequency, because, all other things being equal, people read common words more quickly than rare words. If it happened that the materials were biased, so that the question sentences contained more common words, any difference in reading time could be due to word frequency rather than sentence type. For instance, if participants read the question sentences more quickly, this could be either because they were in the form of questions, or because they contained more high frequency words, or a combination of both explanations. We could not be certain which conclusion to draw.

In a situation such as this, the **conditions** of the experiment differ systematically in more than one way. One condition involves question sentences and high frequency words. The other involves statements and more low frequency words. The two variables, sentence type and word frequency, are said to be **confounded** because it is impossible to decide which is responsible for any difference in the **dependent variable**.

Another common problem with materials arises if the materials are already known to participants. In many studies, especially in cognitive psychology, investigators aim to examine the reasoning processes and inferences people make when they tackle new situations. For example, in problem solving studies, participants are given puzzles to solve, and investigators examine the effect of variables such as whether the problem is expressed in concrete terms or abstractly. However, if the problem is one the participant already knows the answer to, they can solve it just by retrieving the answer from memory. For instance, if I give you the arithmetic problem "5 + 3 = ?", you can probably answer "8" without having to do any mental arithmetic, you just remember that the answer is 8.

A related problem affects tests and questionnaires which are administered more than once to the same participants. Obviously, we can expect the first test to influence responses to the second, and this influence can take different forms. Most simply, participants are likely to benefit from practice and greater familiarity with the items and the test format. Another possibility is that, on the second occasion, participants respond by recalling their answer to the first test. For example, I could ask you how many hours you spent eating on your last birthday. If I ask you now, you will probably work out a response by trying to recall what you did during your last birthday. However, if I ask you again in an hour, you may not bother going through that process. You might, instead, shortcut the process and simply repeat the answer you gave the first time, at least, as well as you can remember it an hour later. Conversely, participants might respond by choosing to give a different answer to the one they initially gave. This is more likely if the second time of asking is very soon after the first, and has been found to be a problem in developmental research. If a child is asked the same question again, they may reasonably guess that the first answer must not have been the answer that was desired.

Researchers avoid the problems of repeated testing in two main ways. First, they sometimes redesign experiments so that the test or question is posed only once. Second, they devise alternative forms of a test, sometimes called **parallel forms**. At the second testing, a different version of the test is given. The parallel form is designed to measure the same **constructs**, with the same level of reliability and validity, but with different items.

Participants will try to work out the intended meaning of questions they are asked, but they may not always interpret things the way the experimenter meant them to be interpreted. This is a particular issue in the design of questionnaires and surveys, but affects instructions in experiments as well.

A straightforward example is when the experimenter uses a technical term in a question. For example, an experimenter researching emotions might show participants an image, and ask "Does this make you feel anxious or depressed?". In psychopathology, these terms have a specific definition. The experimenter cannot rely on participants to apply the same definition.

A common problem is when the wording of a question is simply unclear or open to misinterpretation. This can be because the wording is vague. For example, if I ask "How many times have you washed your hair recently?", it is difficult for you to be sure what I mean by "recently." If some participants interpret the question as referring to the last couple of days, and others as the last few months, it will be impossible to compare their answers in a meaningful way. For instance, if I asked 10 boys and 10 girls, and they all said "two times," I could not be sure if boys and girls wash their hair equally frequently, or interpreted the word "recently" in different ways.

There can be more subtle problems with language. One problem that survey researchers noticed many years ago is that if you ask questions in a different order, you sometimes get different answers. One of the original examples was a pair of questions about letting journalists from overseas visit:

1. *Do you think journalists from communist Russia should be allowed to come to the United States and report freely on what they see?*
2. *Do you think journalists from the United States should be allowed to go to communist Russia and report freely on what they see?*

In the 1950s, American participants were much more likely to answer "yes" to question (1) if it was asked second. More detailed discussion of issues connected to the wording of survey questions can be found in Tourangeau, Rips & Rasinksi (2000).

Materials can also become dated as society changes. For example, the following item appears on a **scale** devised to measure a personality **trait** called ethnocentrism. I have to confess, I have no idea what a zootsuiter is. In developing their questionnaire, to which we return in one of the case studies, Adorno et al. themselves dropped items that became dated because the items alluded to specific events that had occurred in the mid-1940s.

"Zootsuiters prove that when people of their type have too much money and freedom, they just cause trouble." (Adorno et al., 1950, p. 128)

THE PROCEDURE

The way the task is presented to participants can affect the results. In this section, we discuss two main issues. First we look at **experimenter effects**. These are ways in which the behavior, or even just the presence of the experimenter can influence participant responses. The second issue relates to within subject designs, in which participants complete more than one **condition** of the study.

Experimenter effects

There is a risk that the knowledge the experimenter has about expected results will affect the outcome of a study. There are various ways this can happen. Enthusiastic participants may unwittingly try to "help" the experimenter by guessing what the desired outcome is. If the participants then behave according to what they imagine the experimenter desires, this could bias the results. Depending on how well they guess, the results could be biased towards or against the research hypothesis.

Conversely, it is possible for experimenters to unwittingly convey the response that suits their hypothesis. For example, an experimenter may ask a participant which of two options they would choose. If the experimenter unwittingly modulates their voice tone, or makes a gesture when explaining the choices, then that could affect responses. Similarly, if the experimenter always offers choice A first, and choice B second, that may have an effect.

In many studies, the response or behavior of participants is recorded by the experimenter. There is a possibility that the experimenter will be unwittingly biased in making those records. For example, imagine that an experimenter wants to test whether people blink more often when they are telling a lie. Participants are asked to say something that is true in one **condition**, and to say something false in another condition. If the experimenter knows when the participant is supposed to be lying, their count could be unwittingly biased. This is an even bigger problem if the coding of the response involves subjective interpretation. For example, if the experimenter aims to record the number of times a participant says something cheerful, or angry, that involves a subjective judgement.

The first part of the solution to these problems is for the person giving instructions or recording data to be unaware of the research hypothesis, and to be unaware which condition is being tested. A researcher in this position is said to be **blind**. One way to achieve this is to automate the running of the experiment. In many experiments in cognitive psychology, it is possible to present most of the experiment via a computer. The computer presents the trials and records the data, and is not subject to unwitting bias. Researchers have also been able to show in several cases that computer-based presentation of questionnaires gives similar results to paper and pencil presentations. By distancing the experimenter, who knows the hypothesis, from the data-gathering process, problems with experimenter effects can be reduced.

For some studies, however, it is difficult to remove the experimenter. A typical example is where an interaction among people is being recorded and coded into qualitative categories. Someone needs to judge each part of the interaction and classify it, and often that person will be the experimenter. This opens up the possibility of a problem similar to **experimenter effects**, called experimenter bias. For example, imagine an experimenter is interested to know whether certain patterns of communication are more successful. The experimenter might set up a situation in which two people have to talk to each other to solve a problem. The experimenter would record what they say, and code it into categories that reflect the communicative intention of the participant making the utterance. For instance, a participant might say "Go to the left for 6 centimetres," and that would be coded as an instruction. The coding requires a **subjective** judgement. It is not practical to do such coding without using a human being to do it. If the experimenter does it, he or she may unwittingly bias the coding in favor of the experimental hypothesis.

In this situation, three steps can be taken. First, a researcher can be employed and trained to use the coding system. Ideally, then, this researcher is told neither the hypothesis nor the condition each participant is in, at least until after the coding has been done. In this way, the researcher is **blind**. However, this is potentially expensive, and rarely possible for that reason. The second step is to set out criteria for each category in the coding system, criteria that are as objective as possible. For instance, the criteria for identifying instructions could be "Starts with a verb; indicates something for the other person to do." Again, this is sometimes easier said than done. In some cases, it may be hard to provide objective criteria. For instance, the sentence "I would go six centimetres to the left" could be an instruction in certain contexts. Third, more than one person can code the responses independently. Statistics can then be used to quantify the extent to which their coding agrees. If the different coders make similar judgements, then this will at least establish that the coding is reliable.

In certain types of research, the subjectivity of the experimenter is promoted as a positive feature. In such research, psychologists are usually interested to learn about the way people experience certain situations. These researchers use their intuition and subjectivity to try to get inside the perspective of the participant, using the things they say, and sometimes other aspects of their behavior, as a guide. This approach to research, called qualitative research, is widely used outside psychology, particularly in sociology, but also in other fields such as medical research.

Within subject designs

A fundamental issue relates to whether the same participants are used in each condition, or whether different groups are used. When different groups are used, there is a loss of statistical power because the individuals in each condition are different people. This creates variation between the groups that is not due to the **independent variable**, but is due to differences between the people in each group.

A within subjects design has each participant complete more than one condition. This means that none of the differences between conditions can be attributed to differences between the individuals tested in each condition, because they are the same people. However, it also means that there can be differences between the conditions caused by practice or **fatigue effects**. Experimenters who use within subject designs have to be careful to avoid **confounding** practice and fatigue effects with the different levels of the independent variable.

For example, imagine a researcher is investigating whether children find addition or subtraction easier. The researcher makes up two sets of items. The first is a list of twenty addition problems: "$1 + 5 = ?; 6 + 2 = ?; \ldots$," and the second a list of twenty subtraction problems: "$5 - 1 = ?; 6 - 2 = ?; \ldots$". The researcher gives the problems to a group of children, and times how long they take for each list. Each child does both lists, first the addition list, and then the subtraction list. Assume, for the sake of argument, that they are 2s faster for the subtraction list, and that the time difference is statistically significant. Would you accept the conclusion that children find subtraction problems easier? Well, we could not draw that conclusion. It could be that they were faster on the subtraction items because it was the second list, not because the problems were based on subtraction. In other words, the advantage of practising arithmetic on the first list may have helped them do better on the second list, the subtraction items. The design that I described confounds the order of the list (first or second) with the independent variable (subtraction or addition).

A **fatigue effect** occurs when participants are made tired or bored by one condition and so perform less well on later conditions.

Researchers deal with order effects by **counterbalancing** the order of presentation. In this example, the researcher could give half the participants the addition list first, and half could get it second. When researchers counterbalance, they hope that the **order effect** will be the same size both ways. That is, they hope that the benefit of practising with addition is exactly the same as the benefit obtained from practising first with subtraction problems. If that is correct, then the counterbalancing will control the order effects.

There are alternatives to counterbalancing that are useful when there are more conditions, such as randomizing the order of presentation for each participant. For more detail on these methods, see a text such as Shaughnessy, Zechmeister & Zechmeister (2003).

DATA ANALYSIS ISSUES

This book is not about statistics, but there are two or three key issues related to statistics that affect the conclusions that can be drawn from a study. Research in psychology tends to use statistics to work out the probability of getting the observed data if the hypothesis was false. If that is a low probability, then the investigator rejects the view that the hypothesis is false. Conventionally, a probability of under 0.05 (5 chances in 100) is considered **statistically significant**.

Assumptions

Most statistical methods, including non-parametric methods, make assumptions about the data being analyzed. For example, ANOVA assumes that the data in each cell of the design have a similar variance. In general, psychological research appears to be sloppier than it should be in checking assumptions. Many published reports fail to say whether assumptions were tested. If assumptions are not met, there is a risk that the probabilities calculated do not accurately reflect the real probabilities. In many situations the error is small, but it can be large, and you may not be able to tell whether it is large. Testing of statistical assumptions is dealt with in other places (e.g. Dunbar, 1998; Tabachnik & Fidell, 2001). For present purposes, I suggest you place greater confidence in statistics if the investigators convince you that they have satisfied test assumptions.

The critical level

The critical level for declaring a result significant is usually 0.05, or sometimes 0.01. These values arose by accident. There is nothing special or magical about the numbers 0.01 or 0.05. They are simply reasonably low probabilities, and nice round numbers that have acquired a particular status through tradition and habitual practice. Bear in mind that there is very little numerical difference between 0.04 and 0.06. When results fall close to the boundary, it makes sense to treat them cautiously. It makes little sense to treat the number .05 as an absolute dividing line between real effects and effects that do not exist at all. Nowadays, most statisticians would think that it is appropriate to report the exact probability, rather than simply saying whether the probability was below 0.05. When interpreting the results of a study, try to avoid treating the results of significance tests in an all or none fashion. Instead, be sensitive to the difference between probabilities that are clearly significant, probabilities that are marginal, and probabilities that are clearly not significant.

A probability of 0.50 represents a 50 percent chance of getting these results if there is no effect due to the **independent variable**. That is clearly not significant. A probability of 0.06, however, is neither clearly significant nor a clear-cut indication that there is no effect. With a marginal result such as this it is sensible to be cautious. You would not want to accept the hypothesis with confidence. However, it would be unsafe to reject the **hypothesis** definitively. A number of things can make it difficult to get a **statistically significant** result even when there is a real effect. If the measurements are unreliable, or if there are too few participants, it will be less easy to detect effects. It can also happen that measurements are not sensitive enough to differentiate groups of participants. For example, if I compared the intelligence of psychologists with the intelligence of surgeons by asking them to define the words "apple," "car," and "dog," it is unlikely that my measure would be sensitive enough to separate the groups. Likely everyone would get three out of three.

Effect size

It is useful to bear in mind that statistical significance is not the same thing as size of effect. A result can be significant even when the effect is quite small. **Effect size** measures tell you not just whether something makes a difference, but how big a difference it makes. There are two common ways of characterizing effect size. The first approach is based on the amount of variance in outcome scores that can be accounted for by a predictor variable. For example, imagine I am studying soup consumption in cold weather, and my hypothesis is that people drink more hot soup in cold weather. If I correlate the number of bowls of soup sold each day with the temperature, I can test whether there is a significant relationship, and I can also test what percentage of the day-to-day variation in soup consumption is associated with temperature.

The second approach to effect size describes the difference between two groups or conditions. In this approach, the difference is typically divided by the standard deviation of scores, and so indicates how many standard deviations the means of two groups are apart. For example, imagine I follow up my correlational study into soup eating with a designed experiment. I **randomly assign** participants to high and low temperature conditions, and record how much soup is eaten. Again, I can use statistics to tell me how likely it is to get the observed difference in soup eating if temperature does not influence it. If that probability is low, then the difference is said to be significant. I can also use statistics to measure the **effect size**. If I work out how many standard deviations the group means are apart, I will have an indication of how big the effect of temperature is.

Many researchers now report confidence intervals. A confidence interval indicates a range of values within which the population mean is likely to fall. For example, if I report that the 95 percent confidence interval for soup eating in cold weather is 2.6–3.4 bowls a week, what that means is that you can be 95 percent confident that the true number of bowls eaten each week in cold weather lies between 2.6 and 3.4. Confidence intervals can tell you about both statistical significance and effect size at the same time. Let us say that the 95 percent confidence interval in hot weather is 0.2–0.8 bowls a week. We can see that the two confidence intervals do not overlap: the upper limit in cold weather is below the lower limit in hot weather. That means the difference is significant. Since these are 95 percent confidence intervals, we can conclude that the difference is significant at the 0.05 level (1.0–0.95). In addition, by looking at the confidence intervals, we can see how big the effect is: people drink roughly two bowls of soup more each week in cold weather. Finally, confidence intervals can also give you a feel for the quality of a study. All else being equal, a study with better controls, higher reliability, and more statistical power, will tend to produce narrower confidence intervals, and therefore more precise estimates of the true population values.

You will find more information on **effect size** and confidence intervals in statistics textbooks. There are two points to emphasize here. First, bear in mind that **statistical significance** does not imply a large effect size. Results can be significant even when the difference between groups is quite small, especially when sample sizes are very large. Effect size and significance are different things. Second, good quality published research should either report effect size, or at least report enough information that you could calculate the effect size yourself.

Multiplicity

The final point I want to mention on statistics concerns studies that carry out large numbers of statistical tests. This can be a particular problem in exploratory studies that measure many variables, and do not have very specific hypotheses at the outset. For example, imagine a researcher who wants to test whether personality is associated with driving accidents, and imagine that the researcher has no particular theory of which personality variables will be important. The researcher finds 100 tests of different personality traits, and administers the tests to a group of drivers. The researcher then correlates each personality score with the number of accidents the driver has caused. Even if there is no real correlation between any of the personality variables and driving accidents, we would expect five of the results to be significant. Why? Because that is what the 5 percent significance level means: no more than 5 in 100 results would have this big a correlation if there is really no relation. When we carry out 100 tests, we should expect to find the 5 percent. In this situation, we can have no confidence that the significant results reflect genuine relationships between personality and driving accidents.

There are three approaches to dealing with this problem when it arises. The first is to make an adjustment to the statistical calculation to allow for the multiplicity of statistical testing. There are different ways of doing this, but in general they all set a more difficult threshold for declaring a result to be significant. The more tests are done, the bigger the correction. The second method is to cross-validate the result by checking that it is repeatable within the sample tested. For instance, you might randomly split the drivers into two groups, and calculate the correlation for each random subgroup. If it is a real effect, you would expect the result to be significant in both subgroups. If it is a statistical accident, then it is more likely to not be found in both subgroups. The third method is to try to repeat the finding with a new sample. Having detected a potentially interesting correlation in an exploratory study, you run a fresh study designed to replicate the finding. This is by far the best approach of the three I have mentioned.

COMPROMISES

Good research methods allow us to draw clear conclusions. However, good research methods have to be practical, and there are important practical considerations. Every researcher is working with limited resources. There is limited time, and limited money. The research methods used therefore have to fit a budget, and this sometimes leads to a compromise with perfection.

Take for instance the recommendation just made that running a fresh study is the best approach to dealing with problems of multiplicity. It might be the best of the three approaches mentioned, but it is not the least expensive. A similar problem can arise in trying to avoid experimenter effects. We pointed out that experimenter effects and experimenter bias can be avoided by employing research assistants who are blind to the hypotheses of the study. However, this, too, is expensive.

Time is another constraint. Experimenters cannot afford to waste their own time, or the time of research assistants. The more time is spent on one study, the less is available for the next. The time of participants is also important. No one wants to waste their time, and, moreover, if testing takes too long, it may be harder to recruit participants. An example is intelligence testing. The Wechsler Intelligence Scale (WAIS-R) is widely regarded as one of the best tools for assessing intelligence. However, it takes about two hours to administer the full version of the scale, and it requires substantial skill to interpret and score. This is fine when a psychologist is focusing on an individual client in a clinical setting, when it is in the client's interest to receive a thorough assessment, and the results of the test are needed to make potentially expensive choices between courses of treatment. But in the context of a research project, it may not be possible to justify the time and cost, either for individual participants or for the researcher. Shorter versions of scales such as the WAIS-R are available and are widely used. They provide an acceptable compromise in many situations.

THE RESEARCH PROCESS

In the remainder of the book, I present case studies of research projects, and I invite you to consider the conclusions that can be drawn from each. Solutions for each case are given in a separate section in the end of the book. Although in each case I present a single study, one thing I want to emphasize is that research is a process. Each study develops from earlier studies, and leads to new studies. It is rare that a single experiment can completely convince everyone on some theoretical or practical point. Our knowledge and understanding of psychological phenomena is built up through the contributions of many studies.

At the beginning of a research program, observational or exploratory research may be the most useful approach. In these early stages, researchers may still be figuring out what the important behaviors are, still working to identify candidate predictor variables. As knowledge advances, it may become possible to move to experimental designs that permit greater control, and so stronger, more definite conclusions about particular mechanisms.

In selecting the case studies, and in discussing them, I present alternative explanations and criticisms of the studies. Scientific psychology moves forward by testing alternative explanations in new experiments. Sometimes we will see that the original researchers realized that their first studies left a number of explanations open, and we will see how they went on to design new studies that progressively refined their explanation of the phenomenon.

The points in this section are summarized in Table 1.1, which lists several key questions that you can ask yourself about any particular study.

Table 1.1. Key questions to ask when evaluating research in psychology.

Is the research question a good question?
Are hypotheses clearly specified?
Are the hypotheses motivated by a theory?
Does the study make assumptions I can agree with?
Is it possible to answer the research question using the study design?
Does the design permit a conclusion to be drawn about a causal
    relationship?
  Were participants randomly allocated to conditions?
  Was the explanatory variable manipulated by the experimenter?
  Was a plausible mechanism for the causal link specified?
Does the study have a correlational design?
Is it an exploratory study?

Was the sample of participants appropriate?
Was an appropriate number of participants used?
Was the sample representative?
Were participants given any reward?

Are the variables measured well?
Does the study give a satisfactory account of the way measures were
    selected?
Was the reliability of measures reported?
Were standardized tests used?
Have these measures been used in previous research?
Are the measures known to be reliable for the population being tested?
Is there evidence that the measures are valid?
Could the measurements be measuring something other than the target
    construct?
Were any variables confounded?
How were materials (photos, sentences, texts, etc.) selected?
Was the language used to explain the procedure or to ask questions clear?

Could the procedure have biased the findings?
Did the experimenter gather data from participants in person?
Did the person gathering data from participants know the hypothesis?
Did the participants know the hypothesis?
Could the participants have guessed the hypothesis?
Did participants clearly understand their task?
Is there evidence that participants performed the task the way that the
    experimenter intended?
Was the task ecologically valid?
Was the procedure boring or tiring?
Could the participants have had a motivation that affected the results?
Was the study run blind? Double blind?
Did participants take any tests more than once?
Could practice or prior knowledge have influenced performance?

Were data analyzed appropriately?
Were appropriate inferential tests used?
Was allowance made if many inferential statistics were carried out?
Were significance levels interpreted appropriately?

2

CASE STUDIES

1. THE MENTALITY OF APES

In 1924, Wolfgang Kohler published a book with the title "The mentality of apes." In it he described a fascinating series of studies of the behavior of a group of chimpanzees, including Sultan, Konsul, Chico, and Koko. In his experiments, he set out a reward for the ape, but placed an obstacle of some sort between the ape and the reward. For example, the reward might be suspended out of reach.

In the introduction to the book, Kohler describes the following observation, and says that, although it is intriguing, there is a difficulty with it from the perspective of a scientist trying to explain the ape's behavior. Can you identify the difficulty?

A hook is fixed to the ceiling. Through the hook, a string runs down to a high tree branch on the left, where it is loosely tied. The other end of the string hangs down from the hook and dangles in mid-air, out of reach. To that end of the string, a small pail is attached, and in the pail, a reward is placed. Thus, the reward, a banana, dangles above the ape, out of reach.

Sultan is brought in alone. He looks at the basket, but quickly becomes upset, and tries to get the attention of the other apes by beating the fence with his feet. They do not come. Eventually, he turns and quickly climbs the tree. He pauses, looking at the pail, then pulls his end of the string. The pail rises and gets caught against the hook in the ceiling. He lets the string run back through his fingers, so that the pail drops again, before giving it a stronger heave back upwards. This time the pail hits the hook hard enough that the banana falls out. He climbs down and eats it.

When this situation was repeated for Sultan three days later, he did not miss a beat. He went straight up the tree. He pulled the string

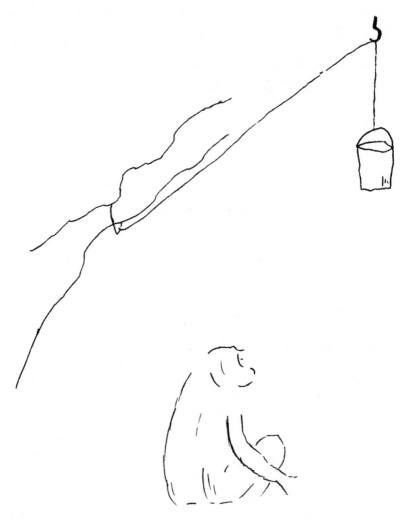

Case 1

twice again, the second time so hard the string snapped. Down came the pail, down climbed Sultan, down the hatch went the banana.

Kohler argued that from this study we see that the ape understood that the key to solving the problem was the link between the string and the pail. However, he finds that the study gives little more information about the ape's thinking. In particular, it does not tell us why Sultan did not simply loosen the end of the string that was tied to the tree. Instead he tugged at it and broke it. Did he not notice that the string was loosely tied to the tree? If he had noticed, would he have been able to realize that it could readily be unloosened? Was it that he did not realize that unloosening it would release the pail, allowing it to drop? Any one of these rival explanations could be correct, and this study does not on its own tell us which. Kohler wrote:

> "So we have performed one experiment which, for a beginning, contains conditions too complicated to teach us much, and, therefore, we see that we must begin the next examination with elementary problems in which, if possible, the animals' conduct could have one meaning only."   **(Kohler, 1924, p. 10)**

Kohler went on to carry out many studies with these chimpanzees, carefully constructing testing situations to build his understanding of how they solve problems. His introductory example teaches us two important things. First, if we want to analyze behavior and understand it, we will often need to construct simplified situations that permit a clear interpretation of different patterns of response. The second lesson is that imperfect studies are often the source of progress and new knowledge. Although this experiment could not answer every question, it did confirm to Kohler that apes can behave intelligently, it identified a situation in which this intelligent behavior could be observed, and it raised interesting alternative hypotheses about how that behavior might be explained.

Throughout these exercises we will be concerned with conditions that complicate our ability to draw conclusions from research.

2. ARE OLDER PEOPLE LESS LIKELY TO MISPLACE THINGS?

It is often said that old people become forgetful with age. Psychologists have been interested to describe and understand changes in memory performance that are due to age. One approach to these questions is to give standard laboratory tests of recall to groups of old and young people, and to compare their performance. However, many researchers have felt that standard laboratory tests have important limitations (e.g. Rabbitt & Abson, 1990). Rabbitt and Abson pointed out that laboratory tasks are usually quite brief, with at most a few minutes between seeing the items to be remembered and then being asked to recall them, while everyday memory tasks require remembering things for hours or days. In addition, people often develop memory strategies to help them cope with the particular demands of their own lifestyle. For example, someone might keep certain things always in the same drawer so that they never forget where they are. These specific strategies may not generalize to laboratory tasks. As a result, those laboratory tasks, while highly reliable, may not provide a valid reflection of someone's capacity to perform everyday tasks requiring memory.

An alternative approach has been to ask people questions about how well they do on everyday tasks requiring memory. A typical question would be "How many times in the last year have you mislaid your house key?" or "How many times in the last month have you walked into a room and then not been able to remember why you went there?" These questionnaires rely on participants giving a "**self-report**," an account of their own experience or behavior.

Tenney (1984) gave a group of older people and a group of younger people a questionnaire about misplaced objects. The percentage that mentioned a recent event in which an object had been lost is shown in Table 2.1.

Table 2.1. Percentage of older and younger participants mentioning loss of an item.

	Younger	Older
Mean age	19 years	71 years
Reported loss of an item	31.3%	26.4%

There was no significant difference in the proportion of the older and younger groups mentioning a misplaced item. In fact, a smaller percentage of the older group mentioned a lost object. Would you accept this as evidence that getting older does not make it more likely that an individual will start losing things?

The solution for this case study is on **page 97**.

3. DO WOMEN HAVE BETTER MEMORIES THAN MEN?

There is a good deal of evidence that women are better at recalling verbal material, such as lists of words, better than men. This advantage is apparent at all ages, and there is some evidence that it holds cross-culturally. Researchers have been interested in whether this advantage holds for other, non-verbal, types of material.

Two psychologists did a study that could be used to test the hypothesis that women would remember visual images better than men (Galea & Kimura, 1993). As part of the study, participants were shown a sheet of paper with over forty line drawings of familiar objects, such as a car, a spoon, and an owl. They were given a limited time to study the drawings before the sheet was removed. Then, after a short delay, a second sheet of line drawings was presented. Participants had to mark those pictures on the second sheet that were in the original set. Women recognized significantly more items than men.

Do you accept this as evidence that women remember line drawings better than men?

The solution for this case study is on **page 99**.

4. ARE PEOPLE IN THE UNITED KINGDOM SMARTER THAN THEY WERE FIVE YEARS AGO?

An organization called Publicis carried out an annual survey of social and economic trends in the United Kingdom, and results for 2003 were reported in the press. This summary is based on press accounts of the study. Publicis reported that people in Britain were smarter than they used to be.

One piece of evidence they put forward to support this conclusion came from an opinion survey of 1,000 people. The participants were asked whether they "felt smarter than they did five years ago." More than a third said they were smarter, and another third said they were the same. Apparently the results were similar across social classes and age groups.

Would you accept this as evidence that people in the United Kingdom are smarter than they were five years ago?

The solution for this case study is on **page 99**.

5. DOES GRAPHOLOGY WORK?

Handwriting is personal. The headstone marking the grave of Olaf Palme, the Swedish Prime Minister who was assassinated in

Stockholm in 1986, is a very moving memorial. It simply bears his engraved signature. Rather like your voice, handwriting seems very individual, and people who are familiar with it identify it with you.

It has often been thought that the style of a person's handwriting will reflect something of their personality. For example, perhaps people with tiny writing are careful and precise in their thinking. Or perhaps they are obsessed with detail. In countries such as France and Israel, handwriting analysis has apparently been widely used in job selection. It is important to know, then, whether handwriting analysis is valid. That is, whether the judgement of a graphologist can accurately predict job success.

Keinan, Barak & Ramati (1984) carried out a study to evaluate this question. A group of six graphologists were given samples of handwriting from 65 candidates for officer training in the Israeli army (19–20 years old). The handwriting was taken from the candidates' files, and was a personal statement they had written as part of the application process, talking about their life so far. The graphologists were briefed on the characteristics required for success in officer training, such as motivation and leadership. They then predicted how successful each candidate would be. The researchers compared the graphologists' predictions to the actual outcomes of training. There was a significant correlation of around 0.26.

Do you accept this as evidence that graphology can provide a valid assessment of work performance?

The solution for this case study is on **page 100**.

6. IS THE SELECTIVE MODIFICATION MODEL REFUTED?

Cognitive psychologists are interested in the way concepts are represented. Various models have been proposed, such as the prototype model and the exemplar model. One area in which these models have been compared is concept combination. A good model of concept representation should be compatible with what we know about the concept that results when two concepts are combined. For example, from a concept of "brown" and a concept "apple," we are able to understand the phrase "brown apple."

The selective modification model says concept combination works as follows (Smith, Osherson, Rips & Keane, 1988).

1. The "apple" concept is a prototype. This prototype consists of a list of features, such as color and shape, with possible values. For example, the possible values for color might be red, green, and brown. Each possible value is scored for how typical it is, and each feature is weighted according to its importance. For example, the possible value red would be scored as more typical than brown.
2. The adjective selects one feature of the noun concept. In the case of "brown," it selects the color feature. It then increases the importance of that feature, and increases the typicality of the possible value that it denotes. Thus color would be weighed more heavily, and the most typical value of color for "brown apples" would be "brown."

This model can be tested by seeing how people rate particular apples as instances of the category "brown apple." For example, experiments show that people will rate a particular apple which is brown as a better example of the concept "brown apple" than of the concept "apple." The selective modification model can account for such data. An apple that is brown matches the selectively modified concept better because its color is the prototypical color, brown.

Some researchers carried out a study to demonstrate their view that the selective modification model was incorrect (Medin & Shoben, 1988). They used combined concepts such as "wooden spoon." According to the selective modification model, wooden should pick out one feature, perhaps the "material" feature, to modify. This group of researchers pointed out that, while a wooden spoon is indeed made of wood rather than metal (which spoons are typically made of) they are also typically of a different size – a typical wooden spoon is bigger than a typical spoon. Thus, in fact, the adjective wooden modifies more than one feature of the spoon prototype.

They demonstrated this by asking participants to rate the combined concepts in relation to test categories. For example, they asked participants to rate, on a scale of 1–10, how typical a "wooden spoon" was as an example of a "large spoon." They found that "wooden spoon" was rated a better example of the category "large spoon" than "metal spoon" was.

Some of the other examples used by Medin and Shoben are shown in Table 6.1. The test categories in each case tested a property not directly denoted by the modifier in the combination. For example, the modifier "color" does not say anything about size. According to the selective modification model, then, there is no reason why the difference between "color" and "black and white" should affect ratings of size.

Table 6.1. Examples used by Medin and Shoben.

The combination . . .	was rated higher than . . .	as an instance of the test category . . .
Wooden spoon	Metal spoon	Large spoon
Color television	Black and white television	Large television
Paperback book	Hardcover book	Fiction book
Cultivated flower	Wild flower	Large flower
Health food	Junk food	Bland food
Small ball	Large ball	Hard ball
Flat roof	Slanted roof	Florida roof
Summer shirt	Winter shirt	Light shirt

Do you accept this as evidence against the selective modification model?

The solution for this case study is on **page 101**.

7. IS THE F-SCALE A VALID QUESTIONNAIRE?

In the 1930s and the 1940s, the fascist government in Germany instituted policies that progressively marginalized Jewish people in society, restricted their freedoms, and began to systematically kill them. Following the war, in fact beginning shortly before the war ended, a group of social scientists carried out some research to try to understand the psychological basis for prejudiced behavior (Adorno et al., 1950). They believed that there was a particular type of person, whose personality predisposed them to be prejudiced, to be fascist. Positioning their approach within a broadly Freudian theoretical framework, they saw this personality as being forged in the social environment, developing as a response especially to patterns of behavior within the family.

Given their understanding of personality as a complex structure, they used a range of techniques to gather data. Early participants were college students, but later participants were recruited from a range of generally white, middle class Americans, though working class groups and even 110 prisoners from San Quentin State Prison were included. Those who were not college students were recruited by contacting groups such as parent teachers' associations, trade unions, and Rotary clubs. Groups were studied through a series of questionnaires that the team developed. These included a measure of ethnocentrism, and a **scale** to measure authoritarianism, known as the F-scale. People who are highly ethnocentric were characterized as tending to reject people from other groups, and tending to do this to other groups in general, who are seen as threatening. They also tend to show high respect for leaders of their "**in-groups**," the groups to which they see themselves as belonging.

In addition, a few individuals were selected for a more detailed individual investigation. These people were interviewed carefully using "special clinical techniques for revealing underlying wishes, fears, and defenses" (p. 12). The researchers wanted to combine the methods of academic psychology with psychoanalytic methods. Individuals who were in the top or bottom 25 percent of scorers on the ethnocentrism questionnaire were selected for this detailed follow up. In turn, their responses in the interviews were used to improve the design of the questionnaires.

Here are two example items from the ethnocentrism scale. Participants rated how strongly they agreed with each item on a six-point scale (−3 to +3), with higher scores showing greater agreement.

1. *Although women are necessary in the armed forces and in industry, they should be returned to their proper place in the home as soon as the war ends.*
2. *A large-scale system of sterilization would be one good way of breeding out criminals and other undesirable elements in our society, and so raise its general standards and living conditions.*

The development of the questionnaires involved giving them to samples of people and analysing their responses. The researchers expected people who agreed with some items to also agree strongly with others. These correlations would characterize the personality structure. Individual items were evaluated for their effectiveness. If they did not correlate at all with other items, they were weeded out.

Later in the research project, Adorno et al. devised a questionnaire to measure a disposition towards ethnocentric beliefs, the F-scale. Their aim was to measure the personality structure without

mentioning minority groups explicitly. They found topics for
these questions in the clinical interviews they had carried out.
In these interviews, topics such as sex, family relations and so on
had been discussed, and the researchers felt these could be connected
to attitudes such as prejudice. The F-scale was organized around
a number personality variables, including "rigid adherence to conventional . . . values," submission to authority, and "exaggerated
concern with sexual "goings on." Items were selected to assess these
variables. Here are a couple of items from the F-scale.

*3. A person who has bad manners, habits, and breeding can hardly expect
to get along with decent people.*
*4. What this country needs most, more than laws and political programs,
is a few courageous, tireless, devoted leaders in whom the people can put
their faith.*

The **reliability** of both scales was assessed using **internal consistency measures**, and was high. The correlation between scores
on the F-scale and the ethnocentrism scale was not expected to be
perfect, because the ethnocentrism scale measured overt attitudes,
while the F-scale was intended to measure something closer to
the underlying potential for ethnocentric beliefs. Nevertheless, the
researchers did expect a high correlation if the F-scale was valid.
The correlation they found was 0.75.

The researchers also administered the new F-scale to two of the
male participants who had been interviewed at length. Their overall scores on the F-scale were broadly consistent with their earlier
scores for ethnocentrism, as would be expected given the high correlation between the two scales. The researchers looked at whether
the things the men said during those interviews were consistent
with their responses to questionnaire items. In some cases there was
agreement. For example, Mack, who was relatively ethnocentric and
had a relatively high overall score on the F-scale, said things about
his plans for marriage that were consistent with an authoritarian
outlook:

> "We're both at the proper age. I intend to work part time [if I get into
> college]. I don't like her teaching; I like to support my wife. I've
> always had that idea. But maybe under the circumstances, that won't
> be fully possible. She is a good cook, and that is an asset, what with
> my stomach condition."   *(Adorno et al., 1950, p. 272)*

However, a few other things that he said were not consistent with aspects of his scores on the F-scale. For instance, he did not give a particularly high rating to the item "Every person should have a deep faith in some supernatural force higher than himself to which he gives total allegiance and whose decisions he does not question." This was despite the fact that in his interview he praised leaders of his in-groups highly, and scored high on other F-scale items measuring "authoritarian submission." Adorno et al. suggested that, "one might say that Mack's submissive tendencies are insufficiently sublimated to permit their expression in abstract religious terms." (p. 275)

Was the F-scale a valid measure of the construct it was intended to measure?

The solution for this case study is on **page 102**.

8. DOES REPRESSION CAUSE PSYCHOLOGICAL ILLNESS?

In 1895, Breuer and Freud published *Studies on Hysteria*. This book described a small number of cases in great detail, and presented some key ideas that subsequently played a central role in the development of psychoanalytic theory. Each case described the symptoms of a person suffering from a form of psychological illness. These patients typically suffered from physical symptoms that appeared to arise from psychological disturbance rather than from a physical **pathology**. The case histories also described the forms of treatment applied, and the central finding was that a process that Breuer and Freud termed catharsis led to relief from the symptoms.

We will look now at two of the cases. The question we want to consider is whether the evidence of these cases gives good grounds to accept the explanation put forward by Breuer and Freud.

The first patient was called Anna O. in the case study, and we will use that name, although her real identity is now widely known. Anna was a member of a wealthy family. Breuer described how Anna suffered from a range of symptoms over a period, including paralysis of her arm, a squint, a dislike of water, speaking only English, and appearing to forget her native German. When these symptoms appeared, Breuer found that they could be removed by getting the patient to talk until she came to a particular memory underlying the symptom. For example, Anna recalled seeing a dog sip from a glass of water, and immediately after remembering that, Anna's dis-like of water was cured. This was only successful when Anna was in a particular **hypnotic state** of mind which Breuer termed "somnam-bulism." Breuer did not normally hypnotize Anna. She drifted into this state on her own, usually in the evening, after sunset.

So, catharsis involves recovering and talking through memories of events connected to a symptom. Another key feature of catharsis is that recovery of the memory should be accompanied by the original emotional feeling.

This treatment continued for several months, with repeated appli-cation of this "talking cure" method. Anna's illness had begun while she had been caring for her terminally ill father. Anna recalled an occasion when her father had asked her what the time was, and because she had been crying she had been unable to read the clock dial. The squint in her eye was attributed to this. Eventually, Anna recalled an occasion when, while caring for her father, she had imagined that he was being attacked by a snake. Shortly afterwards, she had reached under a bush to retrieve something, and mistook a branch for a snake. The paralysis in her arm was traced back to those events.

Anna became determined that her treatment with Breuer should end by a particular date, an anniversary. Breuer reported that by this time she had indeed been cured of all the hysterical symptoms, but remained unwell. Anna was then passed to the care of another physician at a different institution. She eventually left treatment some years later, and subsequently became well known for good works.

The second patient was called Lucy R. Lucy was employed to look after the children of a factory owner whose wife had died. Her symp-toms concerned her sense of smell. She could not smell things, the inside of her nose was not responsive to pain, and she imagined that she could smell burnt pudding. At around the time he was consulted in this case, Freud had stopped using hypnotism to assist the recov-ery of memories. Instead, he used a technique of pressing his hand on a patient's head and insisting that they would remember. He used that method with Lucy R.

At first Freud asked Lucy directly about the smell of burnt pud-ding, and she answered in a straightforward way. The pudding had been burned on a particular occasion. At that time, she had recently decided to go home to Glasgow to care for her own mother, partly because, she said, some of the other servants had been unkind to her.

However, she had a conflicting emotion, because she had promised the children's mother that she would look after her children when she died.

Freud was not satisfied with this. He did not feel it was sufficient explanation. After a little thought, he said to Lucy: "I cannot think that these are all the reasons for your feelings about the children. I believe that you are in love with your employer. . . ." (p. 117)

Lucy replied: "Yes, I think that's true."

Over the next few weeks, the smell of burnt pudding subsided, but did not disappear. Lucy still felt low. Around this time, a physical problem in her nose was diagnosed and treated, and some weeks passed in which she did not visit Freud. When she returned, the smell of pudding was gone, but Lucy now complained that she could smell cigar smoke all the time. Lucy could not connect this to a particular occasion, because men in the house smoked so regularly.

To unlock this puzzle, Freud applied his hand to her head and insisted that she should recall. First, Lucy recalled an occasion when a visitor had kissed the children before leaving. Lucy remembered that the children's father had reprimanded the visitor sharply. After further application of the pressure technique, an earlier, but similar memory was uncovered. On that occasion a visitor had kissed the children, but the employer had blamed Lucy. At that time, Lucy said she still hoped that her affection for their father would be reciprocated, and so this unfair criticism had been a terrible emotional blow.

Two days later, she consulted Freud and he found that the sensitivity of her nose had returned. She was cheerful and happy, and this remained the case when he met her by chance four months later.

Freud explained this in the following way. A psychologically traumatic incident occurs, which the mind is unable to resolve, and which the mind turns away from. The memory is repressed, so that it does not become manifest in the conscious mind. All that is left is a symbolic remnant, such as the smell of burnt pudding. Physical symptoms occur because the unconscious memory is channeled, or converted, into a physical form.

Do these case studies provide good evidence that hysterical symptoms are caused by repressed memories? Are you persuaded that the act of restoring the repressed thought to consciousness, catharsis, cures hysterical symptoms?

The solution for this case study is on **page 104**.

9. DID HIS MOTHER'S UNCONSCIOUS WISH MAKE WILLIE A VIOLENT MAN?

Violence surrounds us. People resort to violence in many kinds of situation, and the fear of violence blights many lives. Explanations for the causes of violence, and views on how it can be prevented, are varied. Snyder & Rogers (2002) examined some ideas from psychoanalytic research on violence, and related those ideas to three case studies of violent behavior.

One view from psychoanalytic approaches is that some acts of violence are acts of preservation of the psychological self. These acts are understood as a response to a perceived threat to the self, and the perpetrator is said to experience a sense of relief when the threat is eliminated. An example of a threat would be an event, physical or psychological, which the person felt would shame or humiliate them (Gilligan, cited in Snyder & Rogers, 2002).

In Snyder and Rogers' review, they discussed the role of childhood neglect and abuse in forming aggressive behavior. These experiences are said to lead to an overstimulated "hyperaroused" internal state that gets in the way of psychological development, and causes the person to be less able to contain violent impulses. Snyder and Rogers cited a **secondary source** that advanced the view that "the unconscious desires of the parent may be critical in determining" whether aggression is directed outwards, against other people or objects, or against the person's own mind "as in psychosis" (p. 241). They also discussed the possibility that the children of violent parents may find that their own violence provides them with a bond to that parent.

The first case reviewed by Snyder and Rogers is taken from a popular book about the life of a man called Willie Bosket. Their article summarizes that book, and here I give an even more condensed summary of their account:

> While Willie Bosket's mother was pregnant with Willie, his father was arrested for murder, and she went on the run to evade capture herself. Snyder and Rogers write that the book describes Willie as "active from the beginning, a mischievous child who looked just like his dad", and Willie is said to have been taught to swear early on by his mother "to gain respect on the street". As he became more violent, it is said, his mother withdrew from him emotionally. She

was involved in abusive relationships with men, and sometimes Willie would attack the man, or set fire to things, including his own clothes, to stop the abuse. At 9 years old, he was ordered by a court to attend a special school for boys. "He felt abandoned and angry at his mother". Between 9 and 21 years, he spent most of his time in institutions as a result of violent behavior and other crimes. At the time Snyder and Rogers were writing, he was in prison serving a long sentence.

In discussing the case, Snyder and Rogers said that Willie might have been "temperamentally hyperaroused" because of the conditions surrounding the time of his mother's pregnancy. His mother, they wrote, was convinced he would be bad and "may have unconsciously wanted him to become his father." Willie himself may have "unconsciously identified with his father," and may have been unconsciously enacting his mother's unconscious wish for him to be his father, and to also act for her, and to be an instrument of revenge on her behalf.

Do you accept the conclusion that Willie's violence was influenced by an unconscious wish of his mother?

The solution for this case study is on **page 105**.

10. DOES MEMORY FADE BECAUSE OF THE SHEER PASSAGE OF TIME?

Over the past twenty or so years, psychologists studying memory have been intrigued by "flashbulb" memories. A flashbulb memory is one that is particularly clear and vivid, and is usually associated with a highly significant event. People often report clear and vivid memories for the moment at which they learned about a sensational event, such as the assassination of a famous politician. They can remember who was with them, who told them, and who they talked to about the event.

An important question is whether these memories really are accurate, and several studies have tried to establish this. To do this, the experimenter needs to be able to establish accurate information, so that the memory can be compared to this. One method that has been used has been to ask people about the event very quickly afterwards. This gives the researcher an almost contemporary record.

Participants can then be asked again about the event some time later. If the memory is good, their answers should agree with those they gave before.

In one important study, Schmolck, Buffalo & Squire (2000) asked 222 college students about the moment they learned that OJ Simpson had been acquitted of the murder of his wife. OJ Simpson had been a famous sports star in the United States, and the events surrounding his wife's death and his subsequent trial had been followed closely by the press. Within three days of the event, students were tested together in a lecture theater. They were asked when they had heard the news, where they were, who was with them, and about other details. After some months, a sample from the original group was tested again with the same questions. Half the sample was tested after 15 months, the others after 32 months.

Shortly after the 15-month follow-up, a second trial involving OJ Simpson ended. This second trial concerned a case brought by his wife's family. A judge decided that Simpson did bear responsibility for his wife's death. This was a civil trial, so the penalty was financial, and Simpson was ordered to pay compensation.

Participants were recruited for the follow-up by mail and telephone. As with any longitudinal study, there was some **attrition**. Attrition means that some of the participants who took part in the earlier testing did not complete the later tests. The 15-month group was approached by letter and 28 of the 52 who were sent letters took part in the follow up. For the 32-month group, 29 were approached by letter, and 13 of these took part. However, a further 24 were approached by telephone, and 22 took part, a much higher **response rate**.

Schmolck et al. classified recollections as "highly accurate" or "involving major distortion". An example of a major distortion would be remembering being in a different place and with different people than had been reported at the original three-day test. In addition, some participants answered that they could not remember. The results are summarized in Table 10.1. There were fewer highly accurate recollections, and more major distortions for the 32-month group. Interestingly, only about 18 percent of those followed up answered "yes" to the question "Have you ever filled out a questionnaire on this topic before?."

Table 10.1. Recollections at 15 months and 32 months.

Delay before follow-up	Highly accurate	Recollection Major distortion	Do not remember
15-month group	50%	11%	21.4%
32-month group	29%	40%	5.7%

One conclusion drawn by Schmolck et al. was that the sheer passage of time between the original event and the memory test is "a major factor determining the frequency of distortions" (p. 44). Does their data provide clear-cut support for this view?

The solution for this case study is on **page 106**.

11. IS DISGUST RESPONSIBLE FOR SOME PHOBIAS?

Generally, we associate phobias with the emotion of fear, but some researchers have suggested that other emotions can underlie phobias. Sawchuck, Lohr, Tolin, Lee & Kleinknecht (2000) were interested in the idea that feelings of disgust are responsible for starting or maintaining certain phobias. In particular, they wanted to explore the possibility that disgust is an important element in phobias involving blood injection injury (BII) and phobias involving small animals that do not attack and eat people, such as spiders. The idea is that blood injuries and small animals concern people because of the threat that they raise of contamination or infection.

To investigate this idea, they gave a set of questionnaires to a large number of psychology students. The questionnaires included items such as the following (these are not the exact words).

1. (Injection phobia scale) If you were to experience having a blood sample taken, how much anxiety would you feel? [0, "no anxiety" to 4, "maximum anxiety"]
2. (Disgust emotion scale) If you saw someone having a blood sample taken, how much disgust or repugnance would you feel? [0, "no disgust or repugnance at all" to 4 "extreme disgust or repugnance"]

The questionnaires were all standard instruments, and the paper quoted good **reliability** statistics for each scale. From the sample of students, the researchers formed three groups according to the criteria shown in Table 11.1. The gender mean is the mean for participants of the same gender. The patient mean is the mean score for people diagnosed clinically with the phobia.

Table 11.1. Criteria for assigning participants to groups.

Group	Spider phobia questionnaire	Avoids spiders	Made dizzy by blood	Avoids medical procedures	Injection phobia scale
Spider phobic	1 SD above gender mean	Yes	No	No	≤ 2 SD below patient mean
BII phobic	≤ gender mean	No	Yes	Yes	≥ patient mean
Not phobic	≤ gender mean	No	No	No	≤ 2 SD below patient mean

Note: SD is the standard deviation.

Sawchuck et al.'s analysis explored correlations between scores on the different questionnaires, and differences between the three groups. They found that people who were in either of the phobic groups had, on average, higher scores on the disgust emotion scale than the group who were not phobic and that people in the BII group had higher scores for disgust than the spider phobia group.

Would you accept that this study shows that an emotional response of disgust causes BII and spider phobias?

The solution for this case study is on **page 107**.

12. HAVE FEELINGS OF DISGUST EVOLVED FROM A NEED TO AVOID DISEASE?

A research study has argued that the emotion of disgust evolved from reactions to disease (Curtis, Aunger & Rabie, 2004). The researchers believe that disgust helps people to avoid objects that might carry disease.

The experiment was conducted on the Internet. The researchers created a web page where people could **volunteer** to participate. Participants first completed details about their age, occupation, whether they had any children, and so on. Participants then saw a series of images, and had to rate each image. They were asked to say how they would feel about touching the object in the picture on a 5-point scale from "not disgusted" to "very disgusted".

Once the participant had clicked the appropriate point on the rating scale, the image disappeared and the next image appeared on the screen. The images showed a variety of things, including people, bowls of liquid, and wounds.

The researchers found that people gave higher ratings to objects that the researchers had predicted would be associated with disease. For example, a bowl of yellow-green liquid was, on average, rated to be more disgusting than an otherwise identical bowl of blue liquid. Women reported higher levels of disgust than men.

Does this study show that people's feelings of disgust have evolved from a need to avoid infectious disease?

The solution for this case study is on **page 109**.

13. DOES THE SMELL OF OLD PEOPLE CHEER YOU UP?

Chen & Haviland-Jones (1999) reported a study to test the hypothesis that smelling the body odor of another person would help relieve feelings of depression. We need to emphasize, as the authors did, that they were talking about small changes in mood, not a treatment for clinical depression. They ran a study to look at the effect of the body odor of men and women of different ages on a sample of undergraduate students.

Odor samples were gathered from 30 people, men and women in each of three age groups. The mean age for each group is shown in Table 13.1.

Table 13.1. Mean age (years) of men and women in each of the three age groups donating body odor.

	Child	Young adult	Older adult
Male	6	23	73
Female	5	20	71

Four of the older men were 74 years or older, the fifth was 58. Donors taped a clean gauze pad to each armpit, and wore it for 8–10 hours. They were told not to use scent or antiperspirant for four days prior to this, though some were allowed to use a "fragrance-free deodorant provided by the experimenter."

Participants donating odor samples were also instructed not to eat food such as garlic or onion that had a strong smell either on the day before collection, or while the pad was in place. Donors were also asked to leave out a clean pad in their home. This pad was intended to absorb ambient odors to control for environmental influences. Two men and five women of varying ages reported that they had eaten onion or garlic, contrary to instructions. Pads that had been used to absorb a sample were stored in the participant's home freezer, normally overnight.

Once collected by the experimenters, the pads were stored in a freezer in the laboratory. They were taken out for testing each day, and disposed of after a few days use. After a set had been disposed of, a new set was taken out.

The 300 participants, college students, first completed an emotion scale containing 31 items. Each item asked the participant to indicate how often they felt a certain way. For example, one item asked how often the participant feels "sad and gloomy, almost like crying." Responses were given on a scale from 1 (rarely or never) to 5 (very often). Each participant smelled just one type of odor, such as older men, or female children. They sniffed a small glass dish containing five gauze pads, each from one of the donors in that group. After smelling this blend of the body odors of five people of a certain age and sex, the participant completed an alternate form of the emotion scale. An alternate form is designed to measure the same thing, to have similar properties of **reliability** and **validity**, but to contain different items. The idea is to avoid asking the same thing twice. They completed the second form about two minutes after completing the first.

Participants also provided some additional judgements. They rated the odor for pleasantness, and estimated the age and sex of the donor. Their estimates of age and sex were not accurate.

The experimenter presenting the glass dish of odor pads did not know which group it came from. That is, the experimenter was **blind** with respect to the experimental condition being tested.

The effect of odor on mood was estimated by carrying out multiple regression analyses. From their analyses, the experimenters concluded that depressive mood was significantly relieved by the smell of older adults, women, and, especially, older women. Table 13.2, adapted from Table 4 in their original paper, shows the mean change in depression score for each type of odor. Negative numbers indicate a reduction in depressed feelings.

Table 13.2. Changes in depression score after smelling different body odors.

Odor donated by	Mean change in depressive mood
Little girls	−2.06
Little boys	−2.08
College women	−2.02
College men	−0.05
Older women	−4.21
Older men	−1.69
Home	−3.09

Would you accept the conclusion that smelling body odor for 2 minutes can relieve depressive mood, especially if it is the odor of older adults or women?

The solution for this case study is on **page 112**.

14. CAN POSITIVE EMOTIONS REPAIR NEGATIVE FEELINGS?

The positive psychology movement has in recent years investigated the role of positive emotions in well being. One key study set out to test the hypothesis that a positive emotion such as happiness can work to undo the effects of a negative emotion

(Fredrickson & Levenson, 1998). That is, the experience of a negative emotion like fear or anger can be repaired if feelings of happiness are aroused.

Participants were 60 female college students recruited on an American campus.

Emotion was operationalized in terms of cardiovascular response. When negative emotions are experienced, heart rate and related measures are affected. For example, when people experience fear, their heart rate increases. Sophisticated equipment was used to monitor a number of cardiovascular variables while participants watched a short clip of film expected to arouse fear. The film showed a man struggling to avoid a fall from a high ledge. Participants were then shown one of four experimental film clips, assigned randomly. One of these films was designed to be emotionally neutral, one was sad, one was designed to arouse amusement, and one to arouse contentment.

The film clips were selected from a collection formed in an earlier study. In the earlier study, people saw the films, and described the emotion they were experiencing. The films selected were ones that people had consistently described as creating the emotion, and had rarely said aroused other emotions. The original film clips were of different lengths, but in this study each film was limited to 100 seconds, and was shown without sound.

Cardiovascular responses were measured throughout the showing of both films and for about two minutes afterwards. ANOVA tests showed no differences in the average cardiovascular scores for the four groups either in the **baseline** pre-test or during the showing of the first, fear arousing, film. The four groups had a similar response to the fear film.

Cardiovascular responses were monitored while participants watched the second film, to see how quickly they returned to pretest levels. Responses were judged to have recovered from fear when the cardiovascular measures fell back to within one standard deviation of that participant's original resting figures, measured before they saw the first film. To test whether the different experimental films had different effects on recovery, the researchers compared how long the four groups took to recover. These comparisons showed significant differences between the positive film clip, and both the negative and neutral films. The positive film produced more rapid recovery.

Are you convinced that this means that positive emotions can affect people by repairing negative feelings?

The solution for this case study is on **page 113**.

15. DO VIGNETTES HELP US UNDERSTAND THE EXPERIENCE OF DRUG USERS' FAMILIES?

A group of researchers was interested to gain an understanding of the experience of people who lived with someone who abused drugs (Miller, Velleman, Rigby et al., 1997). These family members were partners, parents or, in a few cases, siblings, and typically had around six years' experience of their relative's problem drug use. **Semi-structured interviews** were carried out with the family members. Interviews covered topics like the effect of the problem on the family, and how they had coped.

Later, the interviewer summarized the interview in a **vignette**, a 200-word distillation of the key points as perceived by the interviewer. The vignette would mention any themes or patterns of behavior that seemed important, and could also draw attention to similarities between this interview and any other interview. A vignette was "a researcher's account of the relevant or core elements and recurrent themes of a relative's experience, as recorded in the report of the original interview, including such insights, conjecture and comments on the material as the [researcher] might wish to include" (p. 207).

Each interview was summarized in this way by one other member of the research group, who had not met the interviewee. For a few interviews, more than one other member of the team wrote a vignette. Altogether, the six researchers wrote 117 vignettes for 50 interviews.

Midway through the study, two researchers each analyzed the vignettes they personally had produced so far. One researcher's vignettes were mostly based on the factual information recorded, and she identified 34 themes that occurred in two or more of her 26 vignettes. These included positive themes like "learning tolerance," and negative ones like "financial suffering." The second researcher had done 32 vignettes, had described qualities of the family member, such as "loyalty" (positive) or "overprotectiveness" (negative), and had identified 14 recurring themes. This researcher had gone further in making hypotheses about the reasons underlying patterns of behavior. For example, when one partner showed evidence of jealousy, the researcher's vignette suggested that the drug had become like a love rival.

This study used a qualitative analysis of interview responses to try to gain a deeper understanding of the experience of people living with a drug user. Comment on the methodology used in this study, particularly on issues relating to **reliability** and **validity**. Could a study carried out in this way provide useful information?

The solution for this case study is on **page 114**.

16. IS THE "DRAW A FIGURE TEST" A VALID MEASURE OF SEXUAL ABUSE?

A clinical psychologist noticed what she thought might be an important pattern in her interviews with children (Drachnik, 1994). As part of the regular clinical assessment she gave clients, she asked them to take the "draw a figure test." In this widely used **projective test**, the client has to draw a picture of a person. The basis of the test is that aspects of the client's mental life will be projected, unconsciously, into the drawing they construct. If this is correct, of course, it would be very useful, because it could potentially provide access to thoughts and processes that the client may be unaware of. What the psychologist observed was that children who were found to have been sexually abused were likely to have shown the tongue sticking out in the drawing, or to have included a moustache.

The psychologist decided to check all her records to test this hypothesis. She found that of 43 children who were found to have been abused, 14 included the tongue in the drawing, but of 194 who were not abused, only two drew the tongue.

This result was statistically significant. Do you accept that a tongue or moustache in a child's drawing is a sign of sexual abuse?

The solution for this case study is on **page 114**.

17. DO DIFFERENT KINDS OF MATHEMATICS TEACHING CAUSE DIFFERENCES BETWEEN JAPANESE AND AMERICAN CHILDREN ON MATHEMATICS TESTS?

From time to time, surveys are reported that compare the academic performance of schoolchildren in different countries. A number have reported that children in Japan do better than same age children in the United States on tests of mathematical skills. Mayer, Tajika & Stanley (1991) wanted a more precise understanding of the difference between the two populations. They hypothesized that American children would do less well on problems relating to the "execution" of mathematical operations, but would outperform Japanese children on other, more creative, aspects of mathematical problem solving.

Items testing "execution" were straightforward problems such as "$62.3 + 37.8 = ?$." Other processes tested included the ability to solve verbally expressed problems like the one shown below. This problem is designed to test what was termed the translation process, the process of converting each sentence into a mental representation.

Which sentence is correct (a, b, c, or d)?

Dave has four more cats than Sue:
(a) Dave's cats = Sue's cats − 4
(b) Dave's cats + 4 = Sue's cats
(c) Dave's cats − 4 = Sue's cats
(d) Dave's cats + 2 = 5

The other processes were integration (combining sentence representations), and planning the steps needed to solve a problem. The following problem is similar to the example given by Mayer et al. as a test for planning.

Which operations would you carry out to solve this problem?

Sandy had six cats. Two were run over by a truck, but then one of the others had four kittens. How many cats did Sandy have in the end?

The participants were fifth grade students from Southern California ($n = 132$) and Kariya ($n = 110$). They took two tests. The mathematics achievement test (MAT) measured execution skills. The other test measured creative problem solving skills (MP). MAT scores were used to group children according to mathematical ability. MAT scores were higher on average in the group from Japan.

Table 17.1. Division of children from the United States and Japan into ability groups by matching MAT scores.

MAT score	Group assignment	Number from the United States	Number from Japan
11 or over	1	5	77
10	2	5	13
9	3	9	8
8	4	17	5
7	5	27	6
Under 7	Not included	59	6

Table 17.1 shows how children were divided into groups according to their MAT score. For example, children with a score of 11 or higher were placed in Group 1. Five of the American children and 77 of the Japanese children were in Group 1, reflecting the better performance of Japanese children on this test. You might note that the total number of American children according to the table is different from the number of participants reported earlier.

Mayer et al. used these groups to **match** children from the two countries. They then compared children with matched MAT scores on MP, the measure of mathematical problem solving. They found that children from the United States had higher MP scores on average than Japanese children with the same MAT scores. Specific comparisons of particular elements of the MP test showed that this advantage for the American children held only for "problem integration", and not for "translation" or "solution planning."

Mayer et al. interpreted these results as support for what they called the exposure hypothesis, which says that differences in performance are explained by different amounts of experience with that type of question. Pupils in Japan get more mathematics training, and so their overall performance is higher. However, pupils in the United States, they argued, experience more language-based reasoning problems and so, compared to Japanese children with the same MAT score, they perform relatively better on such problems. Mayer et al. recommended an increase in the amount of mathematics teaching in US schools. They also predicted that, once this was done, US students "will excel in applying their basic knowledge in creative problem solving" (p. 71).

Do you think the relative difference in mathematical problem solving is explained well by the exposure hypothesis?

The solution for this case study is on **page 115**.

18. DO MOTHERS CAUSE REFERENTIAL AND EXPRESSIVE LANGUAGE LEARNING STYLES?

Researchers into child language have distinguished between two styles of early language acquisition. These are known as the referential style and the expressive style. Referential children's early words tend to be nouns denoting objects such as "cat," they use single words in early speech, and their pronunciation tends to be more intelligible. Expressive children's early words tend to relate to interpersonal meanings, such as "do it again," a request for an action to be repeated. They use formulaic expressions including inflectional markers in early speech, and their pronunciation tends to be less clear.

There has been interest in whether these styles are inherent dispositions of the child, that would shape their learning of language in any environment, or whether the way parents interact with children determines their style of language learning. An intriguing study by Lieven (1978) investigated whether the way mothers responded to their children's speech was connected to the child's style. She observed conversations between mothers and their children. Here is a summary of her results:

When the child says something . . .

Referential child's mum responds . . .	Expressive child's mum responds . . .
80 percent of the time	*< 50 percent of the time*
often with new information or a question	*often ignoring what child said or using a cliché*

Is this good evidence that a child's style of acquiring language is influenced by the way their mother interacts with them?

Note – inflectional markers are endings placed on words to mark syntactic relationships. For example, in English, the *ed* on the end of *folded* is an inflectional marker of past tense.

The solution for this case study is on **page 117**.

19. DO INFANTS THINK AN OBJECT THAT DISAPPEARS HAS CEASED TO EXIST?

Jean Piaget was a pioneer of the scientific study of cognitive development. Although he studied other areas, such as perception, memory, and moral development, he is best known for his work on logical or deductive reasoning. Starting from observations of children's behavior, and their responses to his questions, he developed a detailed theoretical framework to account for the regular pattern of development that he saw from simpler to more sophisticated forms of thinking. He characterized development in terms of an invariant sequence of stages. Each stage was explained as the acquisition of a mental structure allowing certain types of reasoning.

A central component of the mental structure formed during the first major stage, the sensorimotor stage, was said to be the object concept. The object concept is the ability to think about objects as permanent, individuated entities that exist independently of the events they take part in. Piaget believed that this understanding of objects developed during infancy, and that very young children did not have an understanding of the conditions under which objects continue to exist (Piaget, 1954).

This apparent lack of understanding that an object continues to exist can be demonstrated in a standard task. In this task, an interesting object is shown to the child, and then hidden under a cloth, in full view of the child. At around five months old, infants typically do not retrieve the object in this situation. According to Piaget, this is evidence that the child thinks the object has ceased to exist.

Slightly older infants, nine months old, say, do retrieve an object that has been hidden under a cloth like this. However, they still make a characteristic error called the place error, or AB error. This error is demonstrated in a variation of the hiding game. In this task, two cloths are placed in front of the child, and the child is shown an interesting object. The object is hidden under one of the cloths, "cloth A." This older child will typically pull away the cloth and pick up the object. The experimenter then takes the object again, and places it back under cloth A. The child retrieves it again. Now the experimenter places the object under cloth B. What does the infant do? Piaget found that the slightly older infants search under cloth A, not under cloth B, even though the object had been hidden under B right in front of them.

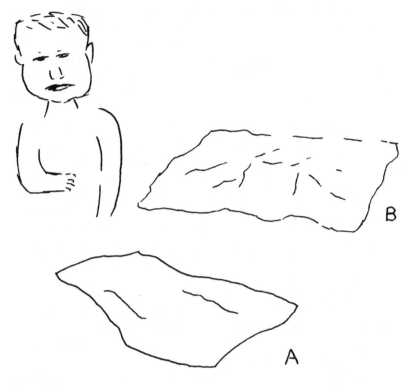

Case 19

According to Piaget, the 5-month-old believes that when the object disappears under a cloth, it ceases to exist. Although the 9-month-old has a better understanding, she has still not separated the object's individuality completely from her own actions. The subjective, or egocentric, perspective of the child dominates. Do you accept Piaget's interpretation of his observations? Can you think of alternative explanations?

The solution for this case study is on **page 117**.

20. CAN INFANTS ADD AND SUBTRACT?

In Piaget's account of cognitive development, true understanding develops gradually. Children may have a partial understanding, but the incompleteness of their knowledge can be revealed in subtle ways by their performance on specific tasks. For example, in the case study "Do infants think an object that disappears has ceased to exist?," we saw that although a 9-month-old would try to retrieve an object hidden under a cloth, she would make the error of keeping searching in the same place if the object was hidden somewhere new. According to Piaget, the logical structure that provides the object concept has still not been completed.

A contrasting view is that in fact logical concepts are more or less innate, and do not take time to develop. Take for instance the concept of number. For Piaget, understanding of number was a relatively late development. Understanding object permanence was a necessary foundation, and on top of that, children would need to develop other mental operations, such as transitivity, before finally achieving a concept of number. (Transitivity is the concept that, if a is bigger than b, and b is bigger than c, then a must be bigger than c. For example, 3 is bigger than 2, 2 is bigger than 1, and, of course, 3 is bigger than 1.)

Wynn (1992) designed a fascinating experiment to try to establish that 5-month-old infants already know how to add and subtract. She used a technique called the startle method to measure children's responses. In her experiment, infants watched a short event unfold on a small stage set up in front of them.

The event on the stage involved dolls being placed on the stage, or removed from it. To test whether children could add, the scene unfolded like this. First, a single doll would appear on the stage. Then a screen would be lifted up to hide the doll. Then a second doll would enter the stage and go behind the screen. The infant could see the second doll arrive, and could see it move behind the screen, but, of course, the infant could not see the dolls once they were behind the screen. Finally, the screen was removed, and it would reveal either two dolls or just one. There should be two dolls, but on half the trials the experimenter surreptitiously removed one of the dolls before the screen was lowered.

The **dependent variable** was the amount of time that the infant spent looking at the final scene. The infant's face was video recorded, and an experimenter who could not see what was happening on the stage timed how long the infant gazed at it. The result was that children looked longer when the scene revealed only one doll.

Wynn interpreted this extra looking time as an indication that the infants were surprised to see only one doll left. To be surprised, Wynn reasoned, they would have to have represented the initial presence of one doll, and the addition of a second. Moreover, the infant would have to be able to calculate that there should now be two objects behind the screen.

Wynn also showed that children looked for longer at an impossible scene following subtraction. In this condition, the stage was initially set with two dolls. The screen rose to hide them, and then one doll was visibly taken away. The screen was lowered and there would either be one doll on the stage, as we should expect, or, mystifyingly, two. Children stared for longer in the latter case.

This general pattern of results has been replicated by other researchers a number of times. Do you accept the conclusion that 5-month-old infants can add and subtract?

The solution for this case study is on **page 118**.

21. DO CHILDREN UNDER 2 YEARS OLD TRY TO INFLUENCE OTHER PEOPLE'S MINDS?

Roberta Golinkoff made an observation of her son's behavior that intrigued her. He was just under 2 years old. The boy had banged his head as he was climbing off a toy giraffe. He touched his head and said "mmm," but his mother did not understand. He persisted, repeating the gesture and the vocalization. Eventually, she realized what had happened and said, "Oh, Jordan hit his head on the chair." This satisfied Jordan, who returned to his play and stopped signalling.

It seemed to Golinkoff that Jordan was trying to communicate, and that his goal was to influence his mother's understanding. He had repeated his signals until she showed that she understood. This would imply that he had a belief, at some level, that his mother had a mind that could be influenced. Of course, the psychologist realized that a conclusion like that could not be drawn from **anecdotal evidence**, and so she designed a study to investigate the hypothesis (Golinkoff, 1986).

Golinkoff observed three children (aged between 13 months and 20 months) communicating with their mothers over lunch. Each child was observed on three separate occasions. One type of interaction she termed "negotiations." In negotiations, which were quite frequent, the child's initial attempt to communicate was unsuccessful, but the child often either repeated the utterance, perhaps with emphasis or additional gestures, or used a different expression, to get the message across. Here is an example given in the paper:

> The child stretched their arm and pointed towards the table. Mother had not understood, and asked, "What do you want?" The child maintained her gesture towards the table. Mother picked up an item of food and asked "This?". The child dropped the gesture, accepted the food.

During this negotiation, the infant makes what the investigator classified as a "repair." In this case, the repair occurs when the child repeats the gesture with her arm. Mother has not understood immediately, and the child tries again. Over a quarter of infants' turns in the conversations were occupied with repairs like these. Would you accept this as evidence that infants believe that other people have minds, capable of understanding, or misunderstanding the message?

The solution for this case study is on **page 119**.

22. CAN TALKING TO SOMEONE WHO IS LESS RACIST INFLUENCE PREJUDICE?

Two Canadian researchers carried out a study to examine whether children's views on other races could be influenced by talking to other children (Aboud & Doyle, 1996). They gave a test of racial attitudes to 88 children aged between 8 and 11 years. The children were from three schools in the Montreal area, and around one third of the children were French speakers. All were described as white, and parents gave written permission for them to participate.

The test was called the Multi-response Racial Attitude test (MRA). Three boxes were placed in front of the child being tested. Each box stood for a different child: one each for a white, black, and Chinese child. On each trial, the child being tested was given three cards, each with the same attribute printed on it. For example, the three cards might have the word "bossy" printed on them. The experimenter asked which of the children were "bossy": ". . . is it the white child, the black child, the Chinese child, or more than one of them who is bossy?" The child being tested gave a card to each of the imaginary children that they thought was bossy. This was repeated for 20 attributes altogether, 10 negative attributes, such as "bossy," and 10 positive attributes. The experimenter then counted how many positive and negative attributes had been assigned to each race, and various scores were calculated.

One type of score just looked at the spread of cards across the three boxes. If children were distributing cards evenly, without regard to race, then they would give out a larger total number of cards. For example, if they gave a negative attribute to just one race (box), then they would give out just one card on that trial. However, if they gave it to everyone, then three cards would be given out. The maximum score by this measure is 3 cards × 20 attributes, i.e. 60. A high score was interpreted as showing more even-handedness.

The other important type of score was called the counter-bias score. The counter-bias score was the total of positive scores for the black box plus negative scores for the white box. Scores could range from 0 to 20, with high scores indicating low prejudice.

Children were split into high and low prejudice groups based on their scores for both these measures, using as a criterion the median score for "same-sex classmates." Those whose score was below the median were assigned to the "high prejudice" group. According to the paper, the two measures correlated ($r = 0.81$) and "were consistent in most cases."

The second stage of the study took place 3–5 weeks later. Each child was paired with someone from the other group. Thus, each child in the high prejudice group was assigned a partner from the low prejudice group. Each pair of children was asked to talk to each other about the way the properties should be sorted into the race boxes. They were given two properties to discuss, one positive and one negative. The experimenters hypothesized that talking to someone who was less prejudiced would reduce childrens' prejudice.

In the final stage, the experimenters took each child into a separate room, and administered a short version of the MRA. This version included 10 items from the original MRA; five positive and five negative. The original MRA scores were then compared statistically to the post-conversation scores. Because the first MRA measure included all 20 items "we halved [those] scores." That would make the possible range 0–10 for the counter-bias score and 10–30 for the total cards score. Table 22.1 shows mean scores on the MRA before and after the conversation for each group. These scores were slightly less extreme after the **intervention** for both groups. The low prejudice group had slightly more prejudiced scores, and the high prejudiced group had slightly less prejudiced scores.

Table 22.1. MRA Scores before and after the intervention.

| | Low prejudice group | | High prejudice group | |
	Before	After	Before	After
Counter-bias score	9.2	8.9	5.9	7.0
Total cards score	26.9	26.2	18.8	21.6

Note: Higher scores are interpreted as showing less prejudice. Scores for before are based on scores for the full test divided by 2.

The difference between before and after scores was statistically significant for the high prejudice group. For the low prejudice group, the difference was not significant with the single exception that on average they distributed positive attributes significantly less widely. Would you accept the conclusion that talking to someone who is less prejudiced can reduce racial prejudice?

The solution for this case study is on **page 120**.

23. DO 4-YEAR-OLD CHILDREN BELIEVE A PERSON'S RACE CANNOT CHANGE AS THE PERSON GROWS INTO AN ADULT?

Hirschfeld (1995, 1996) reported a series of intriguing and fascinating studies of the way children's understanding of the concept of race develops. He has argued that there are two key aspects to this understanding. First, he argued, people are universally predisposed to think of others as belonging to types. People believe these types are inherent and permanent, they are related to biology, and they affect physical appearance and patterns of behavior. These properties are the essence of the concept of race. However, there is a second component. This second component is learned from the society in which a child grows up, and determines how groups are divided into types. These rules about who belongs to a different type arise from social and political relationships among groups, and so are contingent rather than universal. For example, at the beginning of the twentieth century, people in the United States regarded northern and southern Europeans as being distinct racial types, whereas in contemporary US society, that is not a widely held view.

What evidence does Hirschfeld put forward for this view? His evidence comes in the form of some experiments carried out with children, and occasionally with adults. We will look at one of his experiments in this case study.

The experiment concerns children's beliefs about the inherent nature of race. Some previous studies had found that young children believed that if a person's skin color changes, then their race changes. Hirschfeld felt that these studies did not give good evidence because a change in skin color is not a common transformation, and so children might be confused by questions about that. He wanted to use a more familiar transformation to see whether children thought racial type is an enduring, inherent aspect of identity. The transformation he chose to examine was growth: As a person grows, and becomes an adult, does their racial identity remain as it was when they were a child?

Three age groups were tested: 3-, 4-, and 7-year olds. Children were shown sets of three pictures. The first picture, the target, was a drawing of an adult. The adult in the drawing was depicted as black or white, as having a large or ordinary body build, and as wearing clothes associated with a particular occupation, such as a police uniform. The other two pictures were drawings of children. The children were similar to the target in different ways. For example, one might have the same racial features, the other the same body build. The participant was asked which of the two drawings of children was a drawing of the target person when the target was a child. The participant was therefore choosing whether racial appearance rather than body build, or racial appearance rather than occupation, provided a stronger link as a person developed from a child into an adult.

"One of these two pictures is a picture of John as a boy. Show me the picture of John as a little boy" (Hirschfeld, p. 102).

What Hirschfeld found was that children in the two older age groups were likely to prefer a drawing that matched the target for race over a drawing that matched it for body build or occupation. Three-year-olds also preferred a race match to a body build match, but, on average, they did not have a systematic preference between race and occupation. These preferences increased in strength with age. Further analysis showed that this was because of an increase in the proportion of children consistently following a race preference strategy.

Two other sets of participants were tested in the same experiment, and they were asked slightly different questions. The second group

Case 23

were asked a question about heritability: "which of these drawings is a picture of the target's child?." The third group were just asked to say which of the two was more similar to the target. For questions about inheritance, children still tended to favor a match of racial appearance, but when the question was just about similarity, participants did not consistently judge the racially matched child to be more similar.

Hirschfeld concluded that, "even pre-schoolers see race as immutable, corporeal, differentiated, derived from family background, and at least consistent with biological principles of causality" (Hirschfeld, 1996, p. 98). Does the evidence of this experiment convince you of that conclusion?

The solution for this case study is on **page 124**.

24. CAN PERSONALITY PREDICT WHO WILL HAVE A DRIVING ACCIDENT?

Trimpop & Kirkcaldy (1997) reported a study designed to evaluate whether personality variables could predict bad driving. They recruited participants in Canada by advertising for volunteers. Their participants were 120 young men aged 16–29 years, who had had a driving licence for an average of 5.2 years. There is a great deal of evidence that young men have a relatively poor accident record and, indeed, 55.8 percent of the sample reported that they had been involved in an accident.

Altogether 13 measures of personality were made, using four questionnaires. The measures included estimates of "risk-taking personality," "disinhibition," "desire for control," "thrill-seeking," and "arousal avoidance." The researchers examined relationships between these variables and a number of measures of driving experience. Measures of experience included the driver's age, how long they had held a licence, an estimate of how far they had driven in that time, the number of accidents they had been involved in, and how many convictions they had for motoring offences.

We shall focus on a set of comparisons the researchers made to test the link between personality and accident involvement. Drivers were divided into two groups: those who reported no accidents, and those who said they had been involved in at least one. The average age of each group was about the same (22.9 and 22.1 years for the accident and no accident groups, respectively). The two groups were then compared on each personality variable using a one-way ANOVA. There were significant differences on five personality variables, listed in Table 24.1.

Table 24.1. Mean scores on five personality measures for groups of drivers reporting no accidents or at least one accident, respectively.

Personality variable	No accidents group	One or more accidents group
Experience-seeking	5.46	6.25
Disinhibition	4.88	5.83
Risk-taking	41.54	45.62
Wish for control	33.96	32.42
Planning orientation	6.08	4.67

Note: All differences between the two groups of drivers were statistically significant ($p < 0.05$).

The researchers concluded that insurance companies could use personality measures to screen potential customers for likely accident involvement. Would you accept their conclusion?

The solution for this case study is on page 125.

25. DO VIOLENT VIDEO GAMES MAKE PEOPLE AGGRESSIVE?

Do violent video games cause people to become more aggressive? Dominick (1984) reported a study that investigated this question. Questionnaires were distributed to teenage children in two high schools in the southeast United States (Georgia). The **response rate** was good, with about 85 percent of the questionnaires being returned, giving a sample of 250, 44 percent male.

The questionnaire asked the respondents to report how long they spent on a range of activities, including watching certain television shows, playing video games in arcades, and playing video games at home. The television shows that participants were asked about were rated as violent or non-violent by the experimenters. The children completed three questionnaires measuring aggressive attitudes and aggressive behavior. They were also asked to say how well they were doing in school, and an estimate was made of each child's **socio-economic status**, using a formal measure based on their parents' occupation. Except for the measures of video game playing, these measures had been used in an earlier study conducted by a different research group, whose focus had been the relationship between television viewing and aggression.

The data were analyzed separately for the boys and girls, since, on the basis of earlier research, it was judged that there might be differences. For both sexes, there was a significant correlation between video game playing and watching television. Those who spent more time at the video arcade tended to watch violent television shows more regularly. For both sexes, there was also a significant correlation between video game playing at arcades and violent behavior. Dominick also reported significant correlations between school performance and the three measures of aggression. When the analysis controlled statistically for the effects of school performance and viewing of television violence, there was still a relationship between time spent at video arcades and violent behavior, but only for boys. There was no correlation between home video game playing and any of the measures of aggression.

Does this evidence support the conclusion that playing violent video games causes boys to engage in more violent behavior?

The solution for this case study is on **page 126**.

26. CAN PLAYING ACTION VIDEO GAMES IMPROVE YOUR ATTENTION SKILLS?

Green & Bavelier (2003) described several experiments testing the hypothesis that playing action video games improves people's attentional and perceptual skills. In action video games, players have to respond quickly to rapidly changing and sometimes unexpected events in different parts of the visual field. Their hypothesis was that playing video games regularly might not just make people better at the games, it might improve general visual attention skills.

The researchers carried out four experiments comparing the performance of video game players with people who did not play video games. Players were people who had played at least four days a week, at least one hour a day, throughout the last six months. Non-players had to have played hardly at all in the last six months.

In each of the four experiments, participants performed a different visual attention task. I will describe one of them. The useful field of view task required participants to concentrate on a mark in a visual display while detecting targets in other parts of the display. High scores reflect greater ability to rapidly detect targets that appear further from the centre of the display.

Green and Bavelier found that regular video game players performed better on all four visual attention tasks. Assume that the visual attention tasks were reliable and valid. Would you accept this result as evidence that regular action video game playing improves visual attention skills?

The solution for this case study is on **page 127**.

27. CAN PEOPLE SCAN A SCENE MORE EFFICIENTLY BY IGNORING THE LOCATIONS OF OBJECTS THEY HAVE ALREADY EXAMINED?

People searching the visual environment for a target object need to be able to select the target from among the many other objects. For example, if I am searching for a red pen on my desk, I need to ignore the other pens, the notebooks, and the plate of chips. Psychologists are interested in working out the processes and representations involved in completing this task successfully.

One observation that has been made is that the task is easier if the target object is completely different to the other objects than if there is some similarity with them. (Researchers term the other objects distractors.) For example, if the target is a red pen, and the distractors are blue notebooks, search is quite easy. However, if the target is a red pen, but the distractors are red notebooks and blue pens, the search will be a little harder. This type of condition, in which the target shares features with distractors is called conjunctive search because the target is defined by the combination "red" and "pen," and neither feature on its own is sufficient to identify the target.

The research considered here investigated the processes involved in searching for a target among a display of distractors (Watson & Humphreys, 1997). It compared complex and easy search tasks similar to those just described. In the harder task, participants had to search for a blue H among a display of green Hs and blue As. For the simple task, they searched for a blue H among blue As. The investigators found that search was easier in the simple condition, in line with previous research.

Watson and Humphreys also added a new version of the conjunctive task. In this new condition, the distractors appeared in two stages. First the green Hs appeared for 1,000 ms, and then the blue letters were added to the display, including the distractor As, and the target blue H. In this condition, there was a gap after the first set of distractors. What the investigators found was that, with a delay, the results were similar to the simple search condition in which participants only had to search blue letters to find the blue H. It was as if people could ignore the first set of green distractors, even though they were still on the display, and could focus only on the blue letters. In a second experiment, Watson and Humphreys showed that the effect of being able to ignore the initial green distractors depended on how long they were shown before the blue letters appeared, and the effect was at its strongest only once the first set of distractors had been displayed for at least 400 ms.

Watson and Humphreys have proposed that a process called visual marking is the mechanism that best explains their results. The locations of the initial green Hs are marked by the visual system, and once they are marked they can be ignored. Can you think of an alternative explanation for the results?

The solution for this case study is on **page 129**.

28. DOES WORD FREQUENCY MAINLY AFFECT THE EFFICIENCY OF PROCESSING AFTER THE WORD HAS BEEN IDENTIFIED?

Many experiments have shown that people respond more quickly to high frequency words than low frequency words. More common words seem to be easier to process. In a typical experiment, a single word is briefly displayed, and the participant in the experiment has to say the word aloud. This is called a lexical naming task. Another common task is the lexical decision task. In this kind of task, participants press a button to indicate whether a letter string is actually a word in their language. For tasks like these, average response times are lower (faster) for higher frequency words.

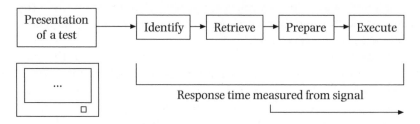

Case 28

There has been some debate about the exact point at which frequency affects lexical processing. Balota & Chumbley (1984) ran an experiment to examine whether the locus of frequency effects lies in the processes associated with identifying the word, or whether frequency effects arise in processes following identification of the word.

At which point in the processing of a stimulus does word frequency affect response time?

In a standard lexical naming experiment, participants are instructed to utter the word as quickly as possible, as soon as they see the word. In Balota and Chumbley's experiment, they asked participants to wait for a signal before they uttered the word. That is, the word would appear on the screen, there would be a brief delay, and then a signal to utter the word would appear. When they saw that signal, participants had to say the word aloud as quickly as possible. The target word remained on the screen until the participant responded.

The delay between appearance of the word and the signal to say it was varied between 0 ms and 1,400 ms. When the delay was 0 ms, of course, the trials were just like a traditional lexical naming experiment.

Mean response times, which I have estimated from Balota and Chumbley's Figure 2 (1985, p. 96) are shown in Table 28.1. Balota and Chumbley found a significant effect of frequency at 0 ms, replicating the traditional finding that responses are faster to high frequency words. Interestingly, they also found this effect at delays of 650 ms and 900 ms. That is, even if people had almost a second to prepare to respond, with the target word on the screen, the response time was still affected by word frequency.

Table 28.1. Mean lexical naming times (ms) for high- and low-frequency words at varying delays.

	Delay		
	0 ms	650 ms	900 ms
Low-frequency words	552	366	355
High-frequency words	491	351	334

Note: Lexical naming times were estimated from Balota & Chumbley (1985, Figure 2).

Balota and Chumbley argued that by 900 ms, the process of identifying which word had appeared must have been long since completed. People normally read over 200 words per minute, identifying and processing around four words per second. Frequency effects found this long after the word appeared, they reasoned, must arise from processes other than identification.

Balota and Chumbley also noted that the size of the frequency effect was just about as large after 900 ms as it was at 0 ms. They argued that, therefore, only a small part of the frequency effect could be due to identification being faster for high-frequency words, and that the "major proportion" of frequency effects in traditional lexical naming tasks must be due to other processes.

Does this experiment demonstrate that most of the effect of frequency is not due to identification processes?

The solution for this case study is on **page 130**.

29. DO THE FIRST AND LAST LETTERS OF A WORD PROVIDE SPECIAL INFORMATION THAT HELPS A READER PERCEIVE THE WORD?

When people read text, they scan along the lines of text. The eye movements occur rapidly in good readers, and consist of a sequence of fast saccades, in which the fixation point is quickly moved from one point on the line to another further on. The point in the text where the saccade lands is thus brought into view of the fovea, which is the central part of the retina with the greatest capacity to discriminate fine detail.

Researchers have been interested to know how the orthographic form of words, the shape of their letters, is processed to allow a reader to identify each word. For example, researchers have wondered whether the first letters provide especially useful information. Studies to investigate questions like this are carried out as carefully controlled laboratory experiments. In the experiments, words are presented on a screen, and participants are asked to read the text. In some studies, the experimenter is able to monitor the eye movements and adjust the display during the experiment. This allows the experimenter to control exactly when the orthographic information becomes available.

Briihl & Inhoff (1995) tested two hypotheses derived from the proposals of other researchers. Taft (1992) had developed a theory that suggested that the "body" of a word contained the most important orthographic information. The body was defined as the first vowel and the consonants that followed it up to the next vowel. For instance, the body of the word "buffalo" would be "uff." The second hypothesis they tested was that the first and last letters, the exterior letter pair, were special and formed a code allowing quick access to lexical identity (Jordan, 1990).

Briihl & Inhoff (1995, Experiment 2) presented participants with text. Just before each word came into view of the fovea, most of its letters were replaced with the letter x. For instance, the word "buffalo" would be transformed to "buxxxxx." Then, just as the word did fall on the fovea, the original letters would all be restored: "buffalo." Participants were usually not aware of any change. The rationale behind this method was that, if the letters first revealed are especially useful, then the word should be read more easily when it is then fixated. The brief preview should help. Any advantage is termed a priming effect, and the initial version of the target word, containing xs, is termed the prime.

Briihl and Inhoff varied those letters that were made available in the prime. Several conditions were compared, in a within subjects design, and Table 29.1 illustrates target stimuli for the conditions that we will discuss.

Table 29.1. Examples of prime and target stimuli in different conditions.

Condition	Prime	Target
Full preview	buffalo	buffalo
No preview	xxxxxxx	buffalo
Body	xuffxxx	buffalo
First two letters	buxxxxx	buffalo
First and last letters	bxxxxxo	buffalo
First letter	bxxxxxx	buffalo

The dependent variables were first fixation time and gaze duration, but similar results were obtained from both, and so we will look at gaze duration data only. Gaze duration is the total time a participant looked at a word before looking at another word. The means (ms) are shown in Table 29.2. Full preview led to significantly faster gaze duration than any of the other conditions. The body preview gaze duration was not significantly different from no preview, which does not support Taft's proposal. Briihl and Inhoff also found no significant difference between the exterior letter pair (first and last letters) and the first letter. From this, they concluded that most of the preview benefit in these conditions could be attributed to the initial letter alone.

Do you accept this study as evidence that the first and last letter pair plays no special role in reading?

Table 29.2. Gaze duration (ms) for target words following full parafoveal preview, no preview, and various forms of partially degraded preview.

Condition	Prime	Gaze duration (ms)
Full preview	buffalo	290
No preview	xxxxxxx	331
Body	xuffxxx	343
First two letters	buxxxxx	320
First and last letters	bxxxxxo	327
First letter	bxxxxxx	322

The solution for this case study is on **page 131**.

30. HOW DO PEOPLE UNDERSTAND AMBIGUOUS WORDS?

How do people understand ambiguous words? The English word "pen" can mean either "a tool for applying ink to paper" or "an enclosure for livestock." On any particular occasion, it has one meaning or the other, and the person hearing or reading must interpret it with the appropriate meaning. People do this rapidly, and appear to do it without conscious effort. Cognitive psychologists are interested to discover the processes and representations that are used to successfully disambiguate words.

Investigators construct models of how disambiguation is performed, and then carry out experiments to see whether the results are consistent with their model. For example, some models say that all the meanings are retrieved, and then the correct one is selected.

Experiments by Swinney (1979) and Seidenberg, Tanenhaus, Leiman & Bienkowski (1982) provided evidence that all meanings were retrieved. In their experiments, participants listened to a text containing an ambiguous word. Just when they reached the ambiguous word, a target word would appear on a screen and the participant had to press a button if it was a real word. This is called a lexical decision task. What these researchers found was that responses to the target were faster if it was semantically related to either of the meanings of the ambiguous word. For example, if the ambiguous

Case 30

word was "bug," people made faster lexical decisions to either "spy" or "spider" than to a word unrelated to either meaning, such as "spoon." Seidenberg et al. varied the delay between reaching the ambiguous word and presenting the target. They found that after as little as 200 ms, only words related to the one meaning that was appropriate received faster lexical decisions. Many researchers have taken these results to show that initially all meanings are retrieved and then, perhaps within 200 ms, the appropriate meaning is selected.

In similar studies, other investigators have discovered an effect called the subordinate bias effect. These studies have measured reading time to estimate how easily each section of a text is processed. Some measure eye movements to work out how long people spend looking at each part, while others have participants press a button to indicate when they have finished reading each part. This latter method is known as self-paced reading because as the participant presses the button, the next piece of the text appears for reading. Studies of reading time have found differences in the processing of the more common and less common meanings of ambiguous words.

For some ambiguous words, the two meanings are equally common, and these are said to be balanced homonyms. For others, one meaning is more common. This more common meaning is sometimes called the dominant meaning, the less common the subordinate meaning. The writing tool meaning of "pen," for instance, is the dominant meaning, because it is more common.

Reading time experiments have found that, when there is no context to help decide which meaning is appropriate, balanced homonyms take longer to read than unbalanced homonyms or words with only one meaning. However, when there is a context and the context supports the subordinate meaning, then the unbalanced homonyms take longer.

One model that attempts to explain these results is the re-ordered access model. According to this model, all the meanings of an ambiguous word are accessed, and there is a race between them to be picked. The dominant meaning has a headstart, but supporting context will boost the appropriate meaning. If two meanings run close to each other, then it will take longer to separate them and pick a winner. With no context, balanced homonyms take longer because both meanings are equally dominant. However, for unbalanced homonyms, if a context boosts the subordinate meaning, then it can run neck and neck with the dominant meaning. When the dominant and subordinate meanings run together, responses will be delayed because it takes longer to choose between them.

There is another model of the way people disambiguate words – the context-sensitive model. According to this model, context can actually select the appropriate meaning of an ambiguous word. The inappropriate alternative meaning is never accessed.

Martin et al. (1999) carried out an experiment to compare these models. They reasoned that if a supporting context can select the appropriate meaning, then there should be no subordinate bias effect in that context, since there will be no competition from another meaning. They also reasoned that the re-ordered access model should predict a subordinate bias effect however strongly preceding context supported the subordinate meaning, since according to that model, both meanings are always accessed.

In their first experiment, Martin et al. measured self-paced reading times for sentences such as (1) and (2), below. The ambiguous word is italicized, and the first sentence has the dominant meaning.

(1) The navigator dropped the compass. He searched the deck *beneath the lifeboat.*
(2) The gambler wanted an ace. He searched the deck *for marked cards.*

They found that in these strongly biased contexts, reading times were more or less the same whether the dominant or subordinate meaning was appropriate. The subordinate bias effect had been eliminated.

When the biasing context was weaker, as in sentences (3) and (4), the subordinate bias effect was detected. This reassures us that the absence of an effect in strong contexts was not due to a lack of sensitivity in the reading time measure or a lack of power in the design.

(3) The mother was in a hurry. She jammed the key *while opening the door.*
(4) The author was clumsy. She jammed the key *while finishing the document.*

Were Martin et al. correct to conclude that these results were not consistent with the re-ordered access model? This is a difficult case. You may find it helpful to sketch the re-ordered access model as a race between meanings. What exactly does the model say is happening?

The solution for this case study is on **page 133**.

31. DID WATCHING A PLAY IMPROVE ATTITUDES TOWARDS SPEEDING?

Road accidents are a serious problem in many countries around the world. For example, in the United Kingdom, over 3,000 people are killed each year, and in the United States accidents involving drivers hitting trees alone account for around 2,000 fatalities annually. Young people, especially young men, are often responsible for accidents. Some believe that this is because young men drive too fast. Two researchers based in England have been developing methods to change young people's attitudes towards fast driving, with the aim of fostering safer driving behavior (Evans & Norman, 2002).

In one study, the researchers used psychological theory to develop an **intervention** that they predicted would lead young people to have more responsible attitudes towards speeding. The intervention involved getting a group of teenage children at a school to design a play based around an accident caused by speed. The play highlighted the potential consequences of fast driving. The group then performed this play for other children of the same age at their school. All of the children completed an attitude questionnaire at the beginning of the study, and again 2 weeks after the play had been performed.

A **control group** of young people at a different school were given the attitude questionnaire at the same time as the teenagers in the first school, both at the beginning of the study, and for a second time at the end. However, the children in the control group did not see the play.

The results were that participants in both schools showed a small improvement in attitudes towards speeding, but that there was a statistically significant improvement only for the teenagers in the first school who had seen the play. Would you accept that these results show that the intervention had been successful, and was worth developing further?

The solution for this case study is on **page 134**.

32. DOES DDAT TREATMENT WORK?

People with dyslexia have specific difficulties with written language and spelling. Many psychologists hold the view that the key problem lies in the cognitive processes that link an alphabetic writing system to the word sound. This is known as the phonological deficit model of dyslexia. Typical interventions to support dyslexic children based on this model involve practice and training in the specific tasks involved in reading.

More recently, an alternative view has been put forward. According to this view, the underlying problem is a poorly functioning cerebellum. Psychologists supporting this hypothesis point to **co-morbidity** with problems of balance and motor coordination. In light of this, a commercial organization based in Kenilworth, England developed a new therapy, DDAT, that aims to improve dyslexic children's reading performance by training their **motor skills**. The idea is that when the basic cerebellar circuits are trained, the specific problems with reading will be resolved. The therapy involves about 20 minutes work each day in which the child practises skills such as balance, throwing and catching, and doing two things at once. The child's family pays the commercial organization for assessment and planning of the therapy, and the parents administer the exercises at home. However, the precise details of the tasks have not been published, and were not given in the paper we are going to consider, because that information is commercially sensitive.

The organization approached psychologists to carry out a scientific evaluation of the therapy (Reynolds, Nicolson & Hambly, 2003). The study took place in a fairly small school in a middle-class area near to the DDAT centre. Children were assessed using a number of measures related to reading ability. These measures were used to identify children to include in the study, and to record their level of performance at the beginning of the study for comparison with their performance after treatment. Children were divided into two groups. The experimental group received the DDAT therapy for six months. The **control group** did not receive the therapy and were not asked to perform any replacement activity because the researchers felt it would not be ethical to ask the families to spend 20 minutes a day on an activity that was unlikely to be helpful. However, after the study had finished, the control group was given the therapy out of fairness.

The average scores for each group at the outset of the study on three variables are shown in Table 32.1. In addition, seven members of the experimental group and five members of the control group were given regular individual one-to-one help with reading at the school throughout the study. The researchers noted that it was regrettable that the groups were not well matched on the NFER measure of reading level. There were 18 children in the experimental group, and 17 in the control group.

Table 32.1. Mean scores (and range) for experimental and control groups on three variables at the beginning of the study.

Measure	Experimental group	Control group
Age	9;4 (7;11–10;6)	9;4 (8;0–10;5)
Dyslexia screening test	0.74 (0.4–1.5)	0.72 (0.4–1.6)
NFER reading test	10.6 months delay (33 months delay – 6 months ahead)	4.4 months delay (45 months delay – 22 months ahead)

Note: Dyslexia screening test scores of 0.9 or greater are considered "at strong risk" for dyslexia, and children with scores of 0.6 to 0.89 are considered "at mild risk." The NFER test indicates how a child's reading compares to the standard for their age. A score of one-month delay means a child is one month behind where they would be expected to be; a score of one month ahead indicates their reading is one month in advance of what is typical for their age.

Altogether, around 20 measures of performance were taken before and after the study for each group. These included school assessment tests, tests of motor skill, tests of reading, writing, spelling, and a test of working memory. There was significant improvement in a number of measures for both groups. For example, mean dyslexia screening test scores fell to 0.39 and 0.44 for the experimental and control groups, respectively. The experimental group showed greater improvement on measures of posture, eye movement, bead threading, and reading, but not on spelling, phonological segmentation, or writing. On this basis, the researchers concluded that the DDAT therapy benefited the children who received it, a conclusion that was reported in the newspapers. Do you think parents would be well advised to accept this conclusion and pay for their dyslexic children to receive DDAT on the basis of this study?

Note. Phonology is the sound system of language; phonological segmentation involves breaking a word into its component sounds.

The solution for this case study is on **page 135**.

33. CAN IT BE ETHICAL TO EAT YOUR PARTICIPANTS?

It is not often an experimenter reports that the participants in the study were sold to a certified butcher. However, in the following study that is just what happened. As you read this summary, think about the ethical issues raised. Do you think the study described is ethical?

Ligout & Porter (2003), two researchers based in Tours, France, wanted to learn more about the ability of lambs to recognize other lambs from their own social group. Earlier studies had found that lambs show a preference for their own twin, with whom they had lived, compared to other lambs of their own age. For example, a lamb bleats less after separation from its mother if it is kept with its twin than if it is kept with an unfamiliar lamb of the same age. This implies that a lamb can learn to recognize its sibling. Lambs can also learn to recognize other lambs if they are kept together for several days.

Ligout and Porter hypothesized that perhaps lambs would show a preference for lambs they had not previously met, but which were related to lambs they did know. Perhaps, they reasoned, a lamb can recognize that a strange lamb looks similar to one they know, and in that case perhaps they will prefer such a lamb to a complete stranger.

The lambs were 16–27 days old, and 24 pairs of twins were used. A few hours after birth, twins were taken from their mother and separated. They were each kept in separate groups in pens with five other lambs, identified by colored markings on their backs.

Two kinds of test were carried out.

Test one

Lambs were taken from their pens and placed in a special testing area. Two lambs were placed in small pens, and a third lamb was released nearby. The third lamb was the the lamb being tested, and it could choose which of the penned lambs to approach.

Lambs preferred to approach a lamb from the group they shared a pen with than a completely unfamiliar lamb, but showed no special preference for the twin of their penmate. These results suggest that lambs prefer a familiar companion, but do not recognize relatives of lambs they know. Interestingly, they did not show a preference for their own twin either. They had been separated from their twin just a few hours after being born, and this suggests that familiarity with their twin had not been consolidated in those first hours.

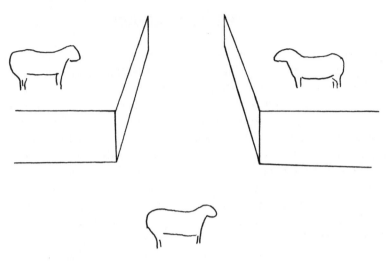

Case 33

Test two

Pairs of lambs were placed in adjacent cages for 5 minutes. During this period, researchers recorded how frequently they bleated, with fewer bleats expected in the presence of a familiar companion. Ligout and Porter compared the number of bleats for a complete stranger, a penmate, the twin of a penmate, or the lamb's own twin. In this test, they found that lambs bleated more with a complete stranger than with any of the others. This suggests that in each of these cases they do appreciate some familiarity.

After the study was finished, the lambs were kept until they had been weaned, and then "either retained for breeding or sold to certified butchers." What ethical issues arise in this study? Do you think the study was conducted in an ethically acceptable way?

Although the focus of this case study is on ethical issues, you can also evaluate the methodology used. In particular, would you accept the experimenters' conclusion that lambs learned the appearance of their penmates and, when they saw twins of those animals for the first time, they recognized the family resemblance?

The solution for this case study is on **page 136**.

34. THE BURT AFFAIR

Sir Cyril Burt was the top educational psychologist in London, and Professor of Psychology at University College London for many years in the twentieth century. He produced a vast body of research on topics related to intelligence, and his conclusions were instrumental in the creation of an examination called the "11 plus." The 11 plus was an examination of intellectual ability taken by British children coming to the end of primary schooling, and the best performers were given an academic education in grammar schools, while the rest had a more technically oriented schooling.

Burt investigated the extent to which innate differences influenced intelligence. He used twin studies to look into the question. In particular, there have been a number of studies comparing identical twins that were brought up separately. Identical twins are genetically identical because they develop from the same fertilized ovum. They are always the same sex, for example. Studies of intelligence looking at identical twins who were reared apart try to look at the influence of genetic inheritance on IQ by correlating the twins' IQs. On the assumption that the separate environments in which they grew up share nothing in common, any correlation in their performance on IQ tests is attributable to their genetic similarity.

Burt's data appear to have been gathered from 1914 onwards, and was reported in a series of papers, including papers published in 1955 and 1966. Even at that time, it was relatively rare for twins to be brought up apart. His sample took time to assemble. The later papers update the results of the first, taking into account data from additional subjects. There were 21 pairs in 1955, and by 1966 there were 53. The twins were given three IQ tests, including one called a group IQ test. Table 34.1 shows the IQ correlations for this test that were reported in each paper.

Table 34.1. Correlations of group IQ scores for identical twins reared apart.

Year published	N	Correlation of IQs
1955	21	0.771
1966	53	0.771

Note: Data from the 1966 paper include the 1955 data.

On the basis of such data, Burt concluded that there is a substantial inherited component to IQ. Do you have any doubts?

The solution for this case study is on **page 137**.

35. DO PEOPLE FROM NORTHERN ENGLAND HAVE LOWER IQS THAN PEOPLE FROM SOUTHERN ENGLAND?

This is a fictional case, but it is analogous to some real research on racial and social class differences in IQ. A researcher was interested in testing whether people from northern England had lower IQs than people from London because of genetic differences. He measured the IQs of men from a mining community near Leeds, and the IQs also of their sons. In addition, he measured IQs of fathers and sons in a small commuter town near London. All participants had been born in the area in which they were tested.

There were two main results. First, in both Leeds and London, there was a significant correlation between the IQs of fathers and their sons. Second, the average IQ score was higher in London than Leeds (about 10 points higher).

Would you accept the conclusion that people from the North of England score lower on IQ tests for genetic reasons?

The solution for this case study is on **page 138**.

36. THE FLYNN EFFECT: IS EACH GENERATION MORE INTELLIGENT THAN THE LAST?

Over the years, IQ test companies have found that they have to keep publishing new test norms. The test norms tell the person scoring the test how to convert a person's test score into an IQ score. The average IQ score is defined to be 100, and to keep it like that, the companies have had to keep adjusting the norms. What is interesting is that they have to do it in the same direction. People keep scoring higher, so the norms keep getting revised to require higher test scores for a given IQ.

Paul Flynn has gathered data from 14 different developed countries on IQ tests at different times in the period since World War II, and earlier in some cases (Flynn, 1987). He has shown that, on average, IQ scores rose by about 15 points between each generation. For example, if British IQ scores from 1942 were converted into IQs on the basis of 1992 norms (average = 100), the average IQ in 1942 would have been just 73.

These IQ gains are found on the "culture fair" parts of IQ tests, like Raven's Matrices. This suggests that the difference is not simply that the younger generations have acquired more knowledge of factual information. These culture fair tests depend heavily on reasoning ability rather than knowing particular facts.

Are younger generations brighter and better than their parents' generation was at the same age?

The solution for this case study is on **page 139**.

37. DO RACE DIFFERENCES IN IQ IMPLY THAT IMMIGRATION TO THE UNITED STATES WILL LEAD TO MORE SOCIAL PROBLEMS?

Herrnstein & Murray (1994) presented an extensive analysis of the relationship between IQ and social and economic outcomes. They based their study in large part on a statistical analysis of data from the National Longitudinal Survey of Youth in the United States of America (NLSY), but they also argued at length on the basis of the findings of other researchers. The NLSY followed a cohort of around 12,000 people who were 14–22 years old in 1979, and Herrnstein and Murray used data collected from them up to 1990, which include information on their parents' **socioeconomic status**, the education and employment of the young person, and, crucially for Herrnstein and Murray "detailed psychometric measures of cognitive skills."

The measure of cognitive skills was in fact the US Armed Forces Qualification Test (AFQT). The US Army wanted to update the norms for the test, which dated back to the 1940s, and had seen the NLSY as an excellent opportunity to norm their test with a large, representative sample.

The researchers looked at several outcomes in turn, and in each case looked at the correlation with AFQT scores, allowing for the socioeconomic status of the young person's family. They reported that lower AFQT scores were associated with low educational success, long-term (but not short-term) unemployment, early marriage, divorce in the first 5 years of marriage, having illegitimate children, having low birth-weight children, a greater likelihood of going on welfare within 1 year of the birth of the first child, having children with behavioral problems and low IQ, chronic welfare dependency, and greater involvement in crime.

The relationships were not always perfect. Herrnstein and Murray divided the sample into five groups (from 5 "very dull," to 1 "very bright") according to AFQT score, and Table 37.1 shows the percentage of each group whose children were among the worst 10 percent for behavioral problems, for white mothers only. The authors noticed the anomaly that 11 percent of the children of the "very bright" white mothers were in the bottom 10 percent of all white children for behavioral problems, and wrote, "The most prudent assumption is that it is an **artifact** of small sample sizes, but the possibility remains that something else is going on, worth investigating in greater detail, with larger samples" (p. 227).

Table 37.1. Behavioral problems and maternal AFQT score.

Mother's AFQT "class"	Percentage of children with worst behavior problems
1	11%
2	6%
3	10%
4	12%
5	21%

Note: Data from Herrnstein & Murray (1994, p. 227).

Herrnstein and Murray then moved on to look at ethnic differences in IQ. They began by reassuring the reader that "even if the differences between races were entirely genetic (which they surely are not), it should make no practical difference in how individuals deal with each other" (p. 270). The criterion for assigning people to ethnic groups was **self-report**: someone who said he is black, or white, was classified that way. They reported that white people scored substantially higher than black people and Latino people on the AFQT in their sample. There were only 43 Asian people in the sample, so a clear comparison was not possible.

The book subsequently considered the consequences of immigration. Herrnstein and Murray pointed out that a little over half of legal immigrants to the United States in the 1980s were black or Latino, broadly understood. What effect would this have on average IQ levels in the United States if the average IQ of the immigrants is the same as the average IQ for their ethnic group? They concluded that probably the average IQ of immigrants would be below the current national average, and so over time, given those patterns of migration, they expected the average IQ of Americans to decline.

The authors considered the argument that immigrants are productive, energetic people, highly motivated to succeed, and perhaps with above average cognitive ability. However, they were not persuaded: This may have been true in earlier years, when there was no welfare in the United States. Those taking the risk of migration would be the most able. However, now "someone who comes here because his cousin offers him a job, a free airplane ticket, and a place to stay is not necessarily self-selected for those qualities" (p. 361). They also considered the Flynn effect, the measured increase in IQ scores in many developing countries. If immigration depresses national IQ, why had the Flynn effect occurred? Why wouldn't the Flynn effect continue to stave off the bleak prospect of falling IQ levels? But this did not comfort Herrnstein and Murray. The Flynn effect was a fine thing, but why should the benefit of rising IQ due to the Flynn effect be held back, "fight[ing] a demographic headwind" (p. 366).

Herrnstein and Murray made some calculations based on an estimate of a 3-point drop in average IQ scores. They estimated that the number of women on welfare, and the number of young people dropping out of high school, would rise by 14 percent, male crime, single motherhood, and childhood poverty would all rise, although divorce and unemployment would not be affected a great deal.

> "The nation is at a fork in the road. . . . Our purpose has been to point out that the stakes are large. . . . In Part IV, we offer some policies to point the country toward a brighter demographic future."
> **(Herrnstein and Murray, 1994, p. 368)**

Do you find Herrnstein and Murray's study of the relationship between immigration and social outcomes convincing, based on the research methods used?

The solution for this case study is on **page 139**.

38. IS SEXUAL REORIENTATION THERAPY EFFECTIVE?

Until surprisingly recently, homosexuality was listed as a psycho-pathology. It was as late as 1980 that it was finally removed from the DSM classification of disorders published by the American Psychiatric Association. Even now, some people, including many therapists, continue to hold the view that homosexuality is a disorder, and should be treated if the person desires treatment.

A number of forms of therapy to change sexuality exist, but there is little good evidence that they are effective. Indeed, professional organizations, such as the APA, while calling for more research, have warned that therapies designed to convert someone from a homosexual to a heterosexual orientation may be harmful. They say that these therapies may lead to "depression, anxiety, and self-destructive behavior" (APA, 1999, p. 1131).

Spitzer (2003) published a study of 200 people who had under-gone reorientation therapies. He recruited participants by adver-tising. He wrote to organizations, often religious groups, and practitioners, who promote such therapies, asking for participants to come forward who felt they had been successfully treated. To be included in the sample, participants had to meet several criteria. They had to say that:

- they were attracted mainly to people of the same sex before therapy began;
- they became attracted to people of the opposite sex after therapy;
- this new pattern of attraction had lasted for at least 5 years;
- they had benefited from the therapy.

Of 274 people who applied to participate, 74 were excluded by these and other criteria. Participants were contacted by Spitzer him-self, who conducted a **structured interview** over the telephone. There were 114 questions, and the answers were either "yes or no," or a rating on a scale. The questions related to two different periods: the 12-month period before therapy began, and the 12-month period preceding the telephone interview. The key analyses focused on the difference between ratings for these two periods.

The mean age at the time of the interview was 42 years for men ($n = 143$) and 44 years for women ($n = 57$). The mean age at which therapy began was 30 years (this age was not reported separately for men and women). Here is some more information about the participants that was reported in Spitzer's paper:

- 93 percent said religion was "extremely" or "very" important to them personally
- 78 percent had spoken in public to support sexual reorientation programs "often at their church"
- 95 percent were Caucasian
- 19 percent were health professionals or "directors of ex-gay ministries"

- 47 percent received their sexual reorientation therapy from a mental health professional of some kind
- 34 percent received it from a religious support group
- 19 percent received it in "other" ways, including for instance "bibliotherapy"

- 44 percent said they were "markedly" or "extremely" depressed in the year prior to therapy
- 90 percent said they had been only "slightly" or "not at all" depressed in the 12 months prior to the interview

Table 38.1 shows the reported changes in sexual orientation and identity for the male participants. The women reported a broadly similar pattern. The sexual attraction score is a rating on a scale from 0 to 100, with high scores indicating that more homosexual attraction was felt. These scores were higher for the period before therapy. The sexual behavior measure is the percentage of respondents saying they had not engaged in homosexual behavior in the relevant period, and this is lower in the period before therapy. The third score shown is the percentage rating the satisfaction they experienced from heterosexual sex at 8 out of 10 or higher. This increases for the more recent period.

Table 38.1. Reported changes in sexual orientation and identity for male participants.

	The year before therapy	The last 12 months
Sexual attraction	91	23
Sexual behavior	26%	99%
Sexual satisfaction	25%	89%

What can be concluded from this study? Would you accept the conclusion that reorientation therapy can produce real change in sexual orientation with no obvious harm to the individuals treated? Does it provide grounds for providing reorientation therapy to individuals who report that they wish to change from a homosexual orientation?

The solution for this case study is on **page 143**.

39. CAN A MEDIUM CONTACT THE DEAD?

Gary Schwartz is a psychologist who has investigated whether mediums can do what they claim to do – contact and convey information from people who are dead. In one study, he compared the performance of a professional medium with a control subject. In this study, the medium carried out a "reading" for someone (the sitter) (Schwartz, Russek, Nelson & Barentsen, 2001). The sitter then rated the accuracy of the reading.

For example, the medium might say "I am seeing a female figure, perhaps a sister or aunt, the month of October is important in some way." The sitter would identify any match that they found apt. For example, the sitter might say "That could be my great aunt Millie, who was married in the month of October." The sitter would then rate the accuracy of the reading. In an example like this, the rating might be "100 percent." Sitters were deliberately selected to be people who believed in life after death.

The task for the control subjects was slightly different to the medium. The controls were students. They did not witness the reading by the medium, or get any report on what happened. They had to answer a series of questions that the experimenters based on the reading by the professional medium. For this example, the questions would be something like:

What relation does the dead person have to the sitter?
In what month was the dead person married?
What was the dead person's name?

The accuracy score for the control **subject** was based on their answers to these questions. If they answered "great aunt," "October," "Millie," they would get 100 percent.

The professional mediums had significantly higher accuracy scores than the controls. Do you accept this as evidence that the professional mediums were contacting the dead?

The solution for this case study is on **page 145**.

40. DOES ALCOHOL MAKE PEOPLE OF THE OPPOSITE SEX LOOK PRETTIER?

In western countries, many young people drink alcohol, and sometimes they end up doing things they later regret. A recent review of the literature on sexual behavior reported that alcohol consumption was linked to less discriminating partner choice (Cooper, 2002). In the context of that review, Jones, Jones, Thomas & Piper (2003) considered three psychological mechanisms that might explain this link.

Alcohol myopia – perhaps alcohol reduces cognitive capacity and so only "highly salient cues such as sexual arousal are processed."

Alcohol expectancy – perhaps people think it is normal to enjoy sex more after drinking, and so they engage in sexual activity.

Facial attractiveness – perhaps other people's faces look more attractive.

Jones et al. wanted to test the facial attractiveness hypothesis. They recruited an opportunistic sample of undergraduates in campus bars. Half were male, half female, and they were told that the study concerned "market research." They were asked to report how much alcohol they had consumed that day, and were divided into two groups of 40: those who reported no alcohol consumption for that day; and those who said they had had the equivalent of between one and six small glasses of wine in the previous three hours.

Participants were shown 118 pictures of faces, half male, in two phases. In the first phase, they were given a preview of all the faces.

Each face was shown on a computer screen for the same length of time. In the second phase, they saw each face again and rated it for attractiveness on a scale of 1–7. During this phase, each face remained on the screen until the rating was given. Drinkers and non-drinkers gave similar ratings for faces of their own sex. However, the drinkers gave higher ratings than non-drinkers for opposite sex faces.

Is this good evidence that the reason for an association between alcohol and indiscriminate sex is that alcohol makes people of the opposite sex look prettier?

The solution for this case study is on **page 146**.

41. DO INEXPERIENCED FOOTBALL PLAYERS PERFORM COGNITIVE TASKS BETTER WHEN THEY ARE TIRED?

Marriott, Reilly & Miles (1993) wanted to know how soccer players' cognitive functioning varied during a game. They compared a group of skillful players, eight members of a college team, to a group of athletes who, although fit, did not compete in soccer or similar team sports. Each participant was tested over three sessions. In the first session, careful physiological measurements were made to establish their fitness level. This information was used to calculate an exercise load for each athlete in the second session. This load was designed to bring each to a heart rate of 157 beats per minute, a level the researchers had previously found was typical for soccer players during a game.

In session two, participants ran on a treadmill for two 45-minute periods, separated by a 15-minute break, simulating the playing time of a soccer game. Participants performed a cognitive task three times: before they began to run, during the break, and again at the end of the second period of running.

The cognitive task involved making judgements about 45 slides, each showing a game situation. Each slide was shown for 20 s, and while it was being shown on a screen, a multiple-choice question was played to the participant over headphones. An example of a game situation would be a picture of a player standing at the edge of the pitch with a defender standing near him. The corresponding question was "Which is the best option for making a pass to this player?," and the five options were "to his left," "to his right," "over him," "another alternative," or "don't know." The researchers reported that the reliability and validity of these items was established by consulting with qualified soccer coaches, but no details of this procedure were given.

In the third session, participants did the cognitive task three more times, again at 45-minute intervals. However, they did not exercise during this session.

Table 41.1. Overall error rates in sessions 2 (exercise) and 3 (no exercise) for soccer players and other athletes.

	Session 2 (exercise)	Session 3 (no exercise)
Soccer players	43.3%	42.2%
Other athletes	47.8%	51.4%

Table 41.1 shows the percentage of errors in sessions 2 (with exercise) and 3 (no exercise). This is the overall percentage for all three attempts at the cognitive task during those sessions. The results indicate that the soccer players made fewer errors than the other athletes, with only small differences in error rate between sessions two and three. Table 41.2 shows the percentage of errors in session two, showing separately the scores for each of the three attempts at the cognitive task during that session. Error rates for the soccer players were lower after exercise than on the first attempt, before exercise began. For the other athletes, error rates were lower at the end of the first half of exercise, but had risen again by the end.

Table 41.2. Percentage of errors at each attempt of the cognitive task in the exercise session.

	Before exercise	During "half-time"	After exercise
Soccer players	49.2%	40.0%	41.7%
Other athletes	49.6%	39.2%	51.9%

Marriott et al. concluded that the initial improvement at half-time for the low skill soccer players "reflects the mental benefits of "warming up" in this level of player" (p. 264), and that the trend was for skillful players to make fewer errors when they were fatigued. Do you agree with these conclusions?

The solution for this case study is on **page 147**.

42. ARE DECISIONS ABOUT PENALTY KICKS INFLUENCED BY EARLIER DECISIONS THE REFEREE HAS MADE?

Football fans love to criticize match referees. Plessner & Betsch (2001) were interested in a particular hypothesis about referees' behavior. They thought that referees might even up major decisions, such as awarding a penalty kick. From this theory, they derived the hypothesis that referees will be more likely to award a penalty kick to a side if they have just denied them a penalty.

Penalty kicks are important in soccer. Matches are often decided by a single goal, and a penalty kick gives the attacking side a high chance of scoring. Plesner and Betch showed a video of a professional match to 58 referees and 57 players. Participants were German, and the match was from Spain. The match was chosen because the video was clear, but the game would not be familiar to the participants.

During the match, there were three possible penalties, as well as other potential fouls. The first two penalty incidents fell to the same team. During the experiment, participants saw a series of 20 clips from the video, including the penalty incidents. At the end of each clip, the experimenter paused the video and participants had to say what decision they would make if they were the referee. Plessner and Betsch wanted to know how responses to the first penalty incident would affect responses to the second: would the participants even things up?

The results are shown in Table 42.1. Thirteen participants awarded the first penalty, and none of them awarded the second. However, 34 percent of those who did not award the first penalty did award the second. A subset of the participants ($n = 43$) were not shown the first penalty at all, and rather fewer of them, only 19 percent, awarded the second penalty. This suggests that the second penalty was more likely to be awarded if the first claim was refused.

Table 42.1. Percentage of second penalty awards.

First penalty	n	Percentage awarding second penalty
Awarded	13	0%
Not awarded	59	34%
Not seen	43	19%

Note: The values for n do not sum to the total number of participants ($n = 119$) reported in the paper's method section.

Plessner and Betsch confirmed a negative correlation between first and second penalty decisions. Participants were more likely to give a different decision the second time. However, the relationship was only found for penalty kicks, and not for minor fouls. (In the original match, the referee awarded the second penalty, but not the first.)

Plessner and Betsch concluded that these results support the hypothesis that when a referee makes a major decision, his decision is affected by earlier major decisions in the same match. Does their study support this conclusion?

The solution for this case study is on **page 148**.

43. IS SUSIE MORE LIKELY TO MOVE TO SUSSEX THAN DURHAM?

A group of researchers recently advanced the hypothesis that people are attracted to live in cities or places whose names are similar to their own (Pelham, Mirenberg & Jones, 2002). For example, people called Flora prefer to live in Florida, and people called Peter prefer St Petersburg.

Their hypothesis was based on a theory from social psychology suggesting that people can boost positive feelings and their sense of self by linking themselves to places, objects, and activities to which they feel an affiliation. The link could involve going to live in a special place, but could in theory affect career choice and other major life decisions as well. For example, someone called "Butcher" would be predicted to be attracted to a career in the meat trade according to this theory. The phenomenon was termed "implicit egotism" by the researchers.

The prediction in this study was, then, that people choose to live in places with names that are phonologically similar to their own name. The prediction was tested in a study of names in states in the southern part of the United States. The researchers got lists of names from a social security database that holds the names of 66 million people who have died in the United States since about 1935.

The researchers considered only states with one-word names, so excluded South Carolina, for instance. From census records, they identified some common first names, whose first three letters matched the first three letters of the name of a state. For example, the names George and Georgina match the state of Georgia by this criterion. Altogether, they identified four states, and for each state, four male and four female names. Table 43.1 summarizes the data they gathered for male names, and is based on their Table 5. The entries in the table show for each state how many people with a particular name died there. For example, 1,477 people called Kenneth were recorded as having died in Georgia.

Table 43.1. Number of deaths of men with particular first names in different states in the United States.

| State | First name | | | |
	George	Kenneth	Louis	Virgil
Georgia	13,697	1,477	1,642	855
Kentucky	11,390	2,092	2,214	1,736
Louisiana	9,100	1,045	5,775	397
Virginia	16,629	2,261	2,332	597

Using the data on the number of people with each name who died, the researchers calculated the number who would have been expected to die in each state if the names had been spread evenly across the states. Using a statistical test, the researchers found that the actual distribution of names did not match the distribution that would be expected if the names had been spread evenly.

There were two potential **confounding** variables that the researchers tried to take into account, age and ethnicity. If people of a certain age were more likely to have been given a particular name, and if there tended to be more people of that age in a given state, then that name could be more common in the state just because of the age of its residents. For instance, if there are more old people in Florida, and old people are more likely to be named Flora, then Florida will on average have more residents named Flora. This would be because of the age of Floridians, not because people named Flora are more likely to move there.

The researchers took account of age by carrying out a separate analysis using data only for people who were born in 1920, who were therefore, obviously, all the same age. The results of this analysis were broadly the same.

Ethnicity could be the source of a confound for similar reasons. If, for instance, a particular ethnic group is more likely to live in Georgia, and if people in that group are more likely to be called George, then any preponderance of people called George would be a result of the presence of the ethnic group, rather than implicit egotism. The researchers controlled ethnicity by focusing only on people with European surnames. They did five more analyses, each looking only at people who all had the same surname, such as Smith, and obtained similar results each time.

The researchers realized that there was another problem with their method. The names they identified from the database would have included people who were born in the state. It could be that Flora is more common in Florida just because mothers in Florida are more likely to give their children the name Flora. To give a strong test of the implicit egotism theory, the study should focus on people who actually chose to move to the state. Realizing this, the researchers carried out another analysis using the names of people who were initially issued their social security identity card in a different state. In the United States, these cards are issued when people begin to work, and so it is likely that someone who was issued the card elsewhere had moved to, say, Florida, in adult life. They again obtained significant results (see Table 43.2), although the **effect size** was smaller.

Table 43.2. Men who probably moved to different states, by name.

| | First name | | | |
State	George	Kenneth	Louis	Virgil
Georgia	3,592	722	657	204
Kentucky	2,570	526	527	299
Louisiana	2,024	411	699	118
Virginia	5,314	964	1,022	198

Note: If the names had been distributed evenly, the chance prediction is that there would have been 3,520 Georges in Georgia, 518 Kenneths in Kentucky, 476 Louis' in Louisiana, and 309 Virgils in Virginia.

Do you accept this as evidence in support of the theory that peoples' implicit egotism leads them to prefer to live in a place whose name is similar to their own?

The solution for this case study is on **page 149**.

44. ARE PEOPLE MORE HOSTILE TOWARDS IMMIGRANTS BECAUSE THEY PERCEIVE THEIR PRESENCE AS A THREAT?

Social psychologists study relationships among groups of people, and an important topic has been the way in which people in one group form attitudes about the members of another group. Florack, Piontkowski, Rohmann, Balzer & Perzig (2003) investigated the attitudes of German citizens towards Turkish immigrants. The researchers expected that if people felt threatened by the migration of Turkish people, they would feel a greater need for security and safety, and this would affect their attitudes towards the immigrants. The specific hypothesis was that people who did not feel threatened would accept the integration of immigrants, with their own traditions, into German society, whereas people who did feel threatened would take the view that migrants should join German society, adopting German ways, should live in Germany but in segregated communities, or should not live in Germany at all.

Degree of perceived threat	Preferred method of acculturation of immigrants	
Low feeling of threat	Integration	Immigrants can live here with their own traditions
Higher feelings of threat	Assimilation	Immigrants can live here adopting our ways
	Segregation	Immigrants can live here in separate communities
	Expulsion	Immigrants should not be here

Note: The term acculturation denotes the processes involved when people start to live in contact with members of a different group or society.

   Participants were 15 women and 206 men, average age 27 years, taking a Chamber of Commerce and Trade occupational training course in Germany that was unrelated to the study. Participants completed a questionnaire. Each item on the questionnaire was a statement expressing one method of acculturation, and participants rated how strongly they agreed with the statement. For example, the expulsion approach was expressed by the statement:

Turks should not be allowed to start a family in Germany. They can do this in Turkey.

The rating scale ran from 1 (completely disagree), to 7 (completely agree). There were four items for each method of acculturation, and the ratings for these four items were averaged so that each participant had a score for Integration, assimilation, segregation, and expulsion. Reliability scores were reported for these measures, ranging from 0.62 to 0.70.

In addition, 15 items were used to assess the extent to which each participant perceived the presence of Turkish people to be threatening. These items took this form:

If I think about the job market, I perceive Turks as . . .

Participants selected a completion for the sentence ranging from 1 (threatening), to 7 (enriching). Scores for the 15 items were averaged to create a measure of perceived threat, which had a reliability of 0.93. Analysis of the data showed that participants who found immigrants more threatening were less likely to support integration, and were more likely to express a preference for assimilation, segregation and expulsion. Does this finding convince you that the level of perceived threat determines people's attitudes towards the acculturation of immigrants?

The solution for this case study is on **page 151**.

3

SOLUTIONS

1. THE MENTALITY OF APES

When we want to test specific hypotheses, experiments need to be designed so that the interpretation of the results is clear and not ambiguous. This solution was given with the case study.

2. ARE OLDER PEOPLE LESS LIKELY TO MISPLACE THINGS?

There are a number of problems with drawing a firm conclusion that old age does not increase the likelihood of losing possessions.

1.   It is always difficult to draw firm conclusions from a finding of no significant effect. It is possible that there is a real effect, but the experiment failed to detect it.

This could happen if testing was not sensitive enough to detect an effect. It could be that the event of losing possessions is not a sufficiently sensitive measure of memory decline to detect a difference between older and younger people. For example, if it is very rare for people to lose possessions, so that few people report losing any, then it will be unlikely that the older and younger groups will show big differences. That would be an example of a floor effect, which occurs when all the scores on a test are extremely low. Another way the experiment could lack sensitivity would be if the age difference between the older and younger groups was too narrow to show a large difference. If the effect of age on memory only happens over 85 years, then the older group in this study would be too young to show a difference.

When there is no significant difference, another alternative explanation that should be considered is that the design did not have sufficient power to detect an effect. Statistical power is a measure of the probability of detecting an effect if there is a real effect. If power is low, there may be little chance of detecting any effect. Power can be increased by increasing the number of participants being tested or by improving the reliability of the testing procedure. Studies in psychology are often criticized for lacking power. So, if you see a reported result of no significant effect, consider whether this might have been because there were too few participants or because there was too much error variance associated with the measures taken.

2.   It could be that older people's memory is so bad that they forget how often they lose things (Rabbitt & Abson, 1996). If the older group were twice as likely to lose something, but half as likely to remember losing it, they would report the same number of lost items as the younger group.

3.   Older people may be more unwilling to give the appearance of having a poor memory. They may therefore adjust their responses downward before reporting them, to avoid giving the impression that they are losing their marbles. When participants adjust their responses to appear better than they are, this is called **impression management** or, sometimes, "faking good."

4.   There could be a cohort (or "secular") effect. **Cohort effects** are differences between groups of people that arise because they belong to different generations, with different types of life experience. People aged 60–70 years at the time of Tenney's study would have been born around 1910, and may have had different experiences of schooling, perhaps with greater emphasis on rote learning. Memory strategies learned in that context could help to mask age-related changes in memory. If later cohorts have not developed the same memory strategies, perhaps when they age the age-related changes in memory will not be masked in the same way, and a difference between older and younger people will be revealed. Another possible difference between the cohorts that is not intrinsically linked to age per se could be attitudes towards possessions. Perhaps the younger group have grown up in times when material goods were more easily replaced or more often discarded, and so have a more cavalier attitude towards looking after them. This, too,

could mask any age-related decline in memory because the younger people would be more likely to lose things for reasons unconnected to memory.

5. Even if a difference between older and younger people had been found, it could be that the difference was not caused by age per se, but by disease. In a sample of older people, there will tend to be a few who have a physical illness that burdens them, or who are suffering from some form of dementia. These conditions are more common among older people. If a few unwell people in the older group are more likely to lose things, then that will raise the average figure for the group. However, the resulting difference between the older and younger groups would not be caused by a direct effect of age on memory.

3. DO WOMEN HAVE BETTER MEMORIES THAN MEN?

The problem with interpreting this result as directly showing that women remember line drawings better was pointed out by one of the authors in a recent book (Kimura, 2003). All the drawings were easily nameable. It is possible that participants used these names when they encoded the items. That is, they may have stored the items as words rather than as visual images. If that is what they did, then any differences between men and women could have been due to differences in verbal recall. This study does not show that women have better memory for line drawings than men.

4. ARE PEOPLE IN THE UNITED KINGDOM SMARTER THAN THEY WERE FIVE YEARS AGO?

Didn't think you'd buy that.

The judgement invited by the question in the survey is entirely **subjective**, and the judgement about both periods (now and five years ago) is made at the one time. It is unlikely that people can accurately remember what they were like five years ago.

A related problem lies in the definition of smartness. Participants could have interpreted this term in different ways. For example, they

might have interpreted smartness as "knowing more about computer technology" or "being able to do mental arithmetic." Different
interpretations could lead to different responses.

These two problems make the data very hard to interpret. Differences in responses could be related to different strategies for
recalling the past, or different interpretations of the question. They
may not relate at all to the question the researchers set out to
investigate.

There is a third problem. The report says that over one third of
people said people were smarter, and one third about the same. It is
not clear from this whether anything more than guessing is involved
in people's answers. If people were randomly choosing between
"more," "less," and "the same," then they would pick each equally
often, one third of the time.

There has been some very interesting work on the design of survey questions in recent years. Tourangeau et al. (2000) discuss the
issues, and describe methods for improving the quality questions
to help ensure that participants and researchers are on the same
wavelength.

Finally, this case study also raises the problem of reporting data
through the media. As far as I know, this study was never published
in a peer-reviewed journal. Though publication in a peer-reviewed
journal does not guarantee that a study is perfect, it is good practice
for researchers to submit work for peer review. This reduces the
chance of poor quality research influencing public debate, and
the format of journal articles ensures that the detailed information
other researchers need to evaluate the work is made available.

5. DOES GRAPHOLOGY WORK?

The first thing to note is that the correlation, although it is significant, is quite low. This means that the graphologists' judgement does
not explain very much of the variance in success on the officer training course.

The second problem, the main problem, is that the handwriting
samples did not only make available information about the handwriting of the candidates. The samples were reflective, autobiographical
pieces composed by the candidates, and each sample would have

contained different details of each individual's life experiences. That information, rather than the handwriting per se, could have formed the basis for the graphologists' assessments.

In fact, Keinan, Barak and Ramati (1984) also gave the handwriting samples to a panel of occupational psychologists experienced in assessing applications for officer training. There was no significant difference in the **accuracy** of predictions by the psychologists, who presumably focused on the content of the message, and Keinan et al. concluded that it was likely that graphologists' judgements were based primarily on content too.

Neter & Ben-Shakhar (1989) reported a detailed review and meta-analysis of research on graphology. A meta-analysis combines the results of a number of different studies to calculate a quantitative estimate of an effect. In this case, they combined the results of several studies of graphology to estimate the true validity of graphology as a predictor of workplace success. They found a small number of studies that had asked graphologists to assess passages of handwritten text that had been copied rather than being composed by the candidate. In this case, the content of the text was not determined by the candidate. The average correlation was −0.01. That is about as close to zero as you can get. This result, though based on only one or perhaps two studies, suggests that the analysis of handwriting per se is not a valid tool for personnel selection.

6. IS THE SELECTIVE MODIFICATION MODEL REFUTED?

There is a problem with the examples of combinations used in the study, such as "wooden spoon." This example is an idiomatic expression, whose meaning is already known through experience. It is unlikely that the meaning of wooden spoon is computed anew from the meanings of "wooden" and "spoon." Participants could simply recall the meaning, rather than working it out. If the meaning is recalled, then the selective modification process is not involved, and the study therefore cannot test it. Looking at the other examples used by Medin & Shoben (1988), many seem to be like this. For instance, people generally are already familiar with color television sets, wild flowers, and paperback books.

7. IS THE F-SCALE A VALID QUESTIONNAIRE?

This study was a major piece of research, and continues to influence discussion and debate within psychology. It tackled an important social issue in a relatively direct way. There can be little doubt that the researchers had a strong personal commitment to this research topic. There is always a risk that, when we tackle a research question that we are passionate about, we will be subject to unwitting biases. The best protection against such biases is to use sound research methods.

It is a great strength of this study that a range of methods was used to gather data. Combining qualitative methods, questionnaires, interviews and **projective tests**, to name some of the methods used, helps to convince others that findings are not specific to just one task, one lab set-up. The aim of developing a set of instruments to measure the full range of elements of personality structure in a reliable way is also laudable.

A potential problem is that participants were volunteers, and were members of particular groups. The authors of the study conceded that their sample could not be described as strictly representative. A representative sample can be made up by stratified random sampling. With this method, different types of people are identified (e.g. male, female, working, unemployed, and so on) and a sample is recruited in which the subgroups have the same relative size that they do in the **population**. For example, if unemployed men are 4 percent of the population, then the researcher would aim to have 4 percent of his sample be unemployed men. The range of types of person involved was broader than is often found in psychological research, and the researchers argued that the potential for good **generalizability** was high.

The wording of the items appears quite dated now. Of course, in the 1940s the items would not have sounded so odd. However, it is worth bearing in mind that questionnaire items can get out of date. If you use an older questionnaire in your own research, it is important to check that the items remain suitable for your participants.

You may also have noticed that all the items point in the same direction. To get a high score on this scale, you answer "yes" to all the questions. Many researchers have pointed to this. Someone might answer "yes" because they do agree with all the questions, or they might answer "yes" just because they prefer to answer "yes." That is, they might be acquiescent, prone to agree, rather than ethnocentric or authoritarian. Subsequently, versions of the F-scale have been produced which reverse the polarity of half the items. For example, question 1 could be rephrased as "A person who has bad manners, habits, and breeding, can expect to get along with decent people." When this is done, in fact quite similar results are usually reported.

Qualitative data from the clinical interviews cannot be regarded as definitive assessments of **validity**, because only two people were considered, but also because we cannot assume, as the researchers appear to, that the **self-report** data given in the interviews are valid. The consistency observed does encourage us to have confidence that the **scales** are measuring something like the beliefs the researchers intended. Nevertheless, it is clear that there are some discrepancies, and the efforts to explain them in terms of incomplete sublimation are little more than speculation.

A further criticism often made is that the theory is too narrow in scope to completely explain prejudice and ethnocentric attitudes. By considering only personality, it fails to give adequate consideration to important effects of the social environment. In some societies, perhaps Germany during the 1930s, or South Africa until the 1990s, prejudice was normal and was embedded in the law and other institutions. In these circumstances, when almost everyone behaves in a prejudiced way, individual differences in personality may not be the key determinant of prejudiced behavior.

I would like to use this case study to make one final point. The summary I have given of Adorno et al.'s project, though longer and more detailed than some textbooks, is still a partial and selective summary. I have selected parts of the story to re-tell because I think they are most relevant and interesting for present purposes. However, there is much more in the original account, much that I have omitted. It is well worth reading original sources, rather than relying on secondary accounts.

Secondary accounts can even be downright inaccurate. Many **secondary sources** have, over the years, reported claims along the lines of "The Eskimo language has 40 (or 100) different words for snow." As Martin (1986) documented, this claim is not faithful to the original sources. First, there is no such language as "Eskimo": The Inuit and Yup'ik people speak a number of different languages. Second, the number of "words for snow" does not appear to be substantially different from the number in, for example, English: a handful.

8. DOES REPRESSION CAUSE PSYCHOLOGICAL ILLNESS?

The first question that has been raised is whether the cathartic method really brings about effective treatment. Particularly in relation to Anna, commentators have emphasized that she was not restored to perfect health under Breuer. Rather, she spent several more years in other forms of treatment before recovering. At best, the treatment may have afforded temporary relief from symptoms.

A second issue relates to the way the memories of events are uncovered. Freud used hypnotism in his early work, but later, from 1892, replaced this with what he called the pressure technique. Clearly there is a risk that either approach could lead patients into giving responses that they think will please the doctor. This **demand effect** could make their memories unreliable. This is especially clear in the case of Lucy R., where Freud actually provided the answer, the patient simply acquiesced.

We know from more recent experimental research that people's recall of events can be greatly influenced by the way the memories are probed. Loftus (1974) showed people a film of a crash involving several cars. Afterwards some participants were asked "Did you see a broken headlight?", while others were asked "Did you see the broken headlight?". The second form of the question presupposes that there was a broken headlight. Participants were more likely to say "yes" to the second question.

Breuer himself wrote of Anna O: "As regards the symptoms disappearing after being 'talked away', I cannot use this as evidence; it may very well be explained by suggestion" (Breuer & Freud, 1895, p. 43). In the case of Anna O, there is also a risk that the patient unwittingly manipulated the doctor. Anna's dreamy states occurred to a regular schedule, and she timed the resolution of her own treatment. Indeed, Breuer was concerned that ". . . her consistency may have led her (in perfectly good faith) to assign some of her symptoms a precipitating cause which they did not in fact possess" (p. 43).

The problem, then, with using these case studies as evidence for repression and the conversion of repressed memories into physical symptoms is that we have no **objective** evidence for the existence of the repressed memories other than what the patient says. However, what the patient says can be influenced by their current desire to please the therapist, to form a consistent narrative, or, even, to bring treatment to an end. Moreover, there is evidence that when an interviewer asserts facts, people may subsequently incorporate these in their own responses. When Freud tells Lucy R. that she is in love with the children's father, he becomes author not only of the theory, but also, almost in the same breath, author of the evidence for it.

9. DID HIS MOTHER'S UNCONSCIOUS WISH MAKE WILLIE A VIOLENT MAN?

There are a number of problems with accepting this conclusion on the basis of the evidence provided by the authors.

First, the account of Willie's life and experiences is second hand at best. It is based on a book by another author. In fact, it is not clear from this report whether that author himself witnessed the events described or met Willie. This means that we do not have a basis for accepting claims like the one that "he felt abandoned and angry at his mother." How do we know?

It is possible that the account of his childhood experience was given by Willie during adulthood, based on his memory of those events. If so, the account given could be inaccurate as a result, subject to the vagaries of memory and **impression management**.

A second problem is that the article does not explain or characterize with any precision the claim that he may have had a "hyperaroused" temperament as a result of the circumstances of his mother's pregnancy. This claim is just speculation.

Similarly, no evidence is given that his mother ever had an unconscious wish, still less that it influenced Willie. No criterion is offered for testing whether a particular unconscious wish is present, and no mechanism is offered to explain the transmission of a wish from the unconscious part of one person's mind to the unconscious part of another person's mind. The postulation of an unconscious wish only appears plausible or useful because it provides a narrative framework connecting the case study with psychoanalytic theories of the mind.

Although there is a useful role in the psychological sciences for case studies of individuals, it is still necessary to demand good evidence for conclusions drawn. In the rest of their article, Snyder and Rogers give some other case studies where they did have first hand contact. You might find it interesting to read their paper and evaluate that other evidence.

10. DOES MEMORY FADE BECAUSE OF THE SHEER PASSAGE OF TIME?

There are one or two key difficulties with interpreting the results of this study.

First, it is anomalous that participants in the follow-up sample, by and large, could not recall the original test three days after the trial ended. The paper does not indicate whether there was any relationship between memory accuracy and memory for the original test. If OJ Simpson's murder trial had been such a key event, why did participants forget they had been asked about it by their professors? Schmolck et al. suggest this poor memory may be because the questionnaire was very similar to normal classroom activity, and so was not distinctive or memorable.

Second, there is a difference in the composition of the two groups. At 15 months, participants were contacted by letter, and only 54 percent responded. At 32 months, 29 were approached by letter and only 45 percent responded. In addition, however, 24 were approached by telephone, and of these over 90 percent responded. One interpretation of this would be that people whose memory is poor are more likely to decline to take part, but find it easier to decline when approached through the mail. When the approach is changed, and 90 percent are recruited, fewer of those with poor memories escape. This is only a possibility, but if it were correct, it could explain why memory performance was poorer in the 32 month group.

We could test this alternative explanation by comparing results at 32 months for those recruited by letter and telephone, but Schmolck et al. did not report the detailed data to let us do that. However, they did ask participants to say how confident they were about their answers. There was a significant correlation between confidence and accuracy at both 15 months ($r = 0.7$), and 32 months ($r = 0.5$). More confident people performed better. This is not a precise test of the alternative hypothesis, but it does indicate that any difference in confidence at 15 and 32 months could be related to the difference in memory performance.

A third potential difficulty was highlighted by Horn (2001). He pointed out that participants tested at 32 months may have confused the two separate OJ Simpson trials. Those who showed "memory distortion" for the murder trial verdict may in fact have been remembering details of the announcement of the result of the civil trial. If this is correct, it suggests that interference from other memories is the cause of poor memory, rather than decay over time. Horn's commentary is worth reading because it makes interesting suggestions about ways to re-analyze Schmolck et al.'s data to evaluate his proposal.

One of the things I hope you will take from this case study is that one piece of research often leads to another. When we question the interpretation of a result, it is constructive to suggest ways of testing whether that alternative interpretation is correct.

11. IS DISGUST RESPONSIBLE FOR SOME PHOBIAS?

We asked whether an emotional response of disgust causes Blood injection injury (BII) and spider phobias. That would be too strong a conclusion to draw from this study. Indeed, Sawchuck et al. emphasized that their's was an exploratory study only, and phrased their own conclusion like this:

> "The finding that BII and small animal phobias are associated with elevated scores on disgust domains unrelated to their phobic concerns suggests that disgust sensitivity may be a generalized phenomenon, operating as a potential diathesis in the onset and maintenance of these fears." **(Sawchuck et al., 2000, p. 759)**

Note, first, that the spider phobia group were not actually "phobic." They did not have scores that would meet a clinical definition of spider phobia, they just had relatively high scores on the questionnaire, compared to other participants of the same gender.

Second, the design is quasi-experimental. Participants were not randomly assigned to be spider phobic or BII phobic. This makes it difficult to exclude other possible differences between the groups. Obviously, however, it would be difficult to carry out the study in any other way. It would be clearly unethical to attempt to deliberately induce phobias in experimental groups. However, studies are occasionally carried out where negative emotions are induced temporarily. Another possibility is to carry out a prospective study, a suggestion made by Sawchuck et al. In a prospective study a sample would be gathered before any phobia develops, and followed longitudinally.

Third, it is not possible to separate the possibility that disgust causes the phobias from the possibility that the phobias cause feelings of disgust. The feelings of disgust could develop after the phobia has formed. Sawchuck et al. did recognize that disgust may play a role in maintaining a phobia, rather than causing it.

Fourth, it is possible that experimenter demand may have played a role. The questionnaire items were relatively transparent. A participant who knew a little psychology, as these students did, could possibly have guessed where the questions were leading. It is also likely that they would have tried to answer consistently. A co-operative participant who answered "yes" to (1) would be likely to answer "yes" to (2) as well, just to give an impression of consistency. Even though the disgust emotion scale included items from other topics, such as disgust at the site of rotting foods, the inclusion of some items directly related to the relevant phobia may have created an effect of this sort.

1. (Injection phobia scale) *If you were to experience having a blood sample taken, how much anxiety would you feel? [0, "no anxiety," to 4, "maximum anxiety"]*
2. (Disgust emotion scale) *If you saw someone having a blood sample taken, how much disgust or repugnance would you feel? [0, "no disgust or repugnance at all," to 4 "extreme disgust or repugnance"]*

The fifth point is related to the interpretation of the items by participants. It is important to distinguish the word "disgust" from the emotion. The emotion can be defined, operationally, by a configuration of physiological and behavioral responses, such as facial expressions, salivation, or feelings of nausea. None of these responses were objectively measured in this study. Instead, the study relies on participants to interpret the word "disgust" in just the right way, the way the investigators intended. We cannot be sure that they were able to appreciate what was meant, and unless participants interpreted the word in the intended way, the questionnaire was not a valid measure of the emotion. This is true even if the questionnaire was highly reliable, as Sawchuck et al. reported. High **reliability** only shows that measures are consistent, it does not show that they are measuring what they are intended to measure. This was noted as a potential weakness by the study authors who recommended that future research should make direct measurements of the physiological and behavioral responses.

To measure disgust, Sawchuck et al. also used a second scale, called the "disgust scale." The authors of the disgust scale have validated their scale in two ways. First, they compared scores on the disgust scale to scores on other measures (Haidt, McCauley & Rozin, 1994). They found, for example, that people with high disgust scores tended to have high scores on a "fear of death" questionnaire. This result shows **convergent validity**: the scale correlates with other measures it would be expected to correlate with. Haidt et al. also wanted to check that their scale was not just measuring concern with self-presentation. They found that there was no correlation with a scale of self-monitoring. This shows **divergent validity**: it is evidence that the disgust scale measure something different to self-presentation. In a later paper, they looked at the relationship between disgust scores and behavior (Rozin, Haidt, McCauley, Dunlop & Ashmore, 1999). People with high disgust scores were more likely to be willing to perform tasks like touching dog food or a cockroach with their lips. This is further evidence that the disgust scale is valid.

12. HAVE FEELINGS OF DISGUST EVOLVED FROM A NEED TO AVOID DISEASE?

There are several issues to consider when evaluating the conclusions of this study. First, the scoring of the dependent variable relies on participants' interpretation of the term "disgust". The experimental instructions offer no definition, and participants have to use their everyday understanding of the word as a basis for their response. No independent or **objective** measure of disgust is made. This casts doubt on the **construct validity** of the study. We cannot be confident that the psychological variable being measured was the **construct** the researchers had in mind. Indeed, we cannot be certain that different participants were recording the same aspect of psychological experience. For example, the difference between men and women could reflect different patterns of interpretation of the word "disgust" or the phrase "very disgusted" by men and women, rather than different levels of emotion.

The second issue is a general methodological problem with Internet research. It is likely that people who use the Internet are not representative of the **population** as a whole. They are, on average, likely to be younger, more intelligent, better educated, and slightly more affluent. They are also likely to have more specific knowledge of computers. The consequence of this is that the results may not generalize well to the wider population.

Concerns about sampling bias used to be raised in relation to telephone-based surveys. When telephone surveys first began, they were criticized because not everyone owned a telephone, and those who did would tend to be on average richer and so forth. However, now that nearly every household has a telephone, there has been greater acceptance of telephone surveys, and it has been recognized that they have advantages over some other methods. For example, telephone surveys can, in certain circumstances, reach people who would be difficult to recruit otherwise, such as the housebound. It is possible that concerns about sampling bias in Internet research will be reduced as access becomes more widespread. Another way of overcoming the problem is to set up representative panels of participants who can then be invited to take part in studies.

A further difficulty with Internet surveys is that the experimenter cannot be sure who is responding. This is in fact true of any survey where the experimenter does not make personal contact with participants. In this study of disgust, participants could enter false demographic information, and there would be no way of detecting it.

Closely related to these two problems with Internet surveys is the possibility that the project was particularly attractive to certain kinds of people. If, for example, people who are relatively neurotic were more likely than others to volunteer to take part, then the results would be systematically biased.

Another general difficulty with Internet surveys is that the experimenter cannot have complete control over the appearance of stimuli. Depending on the version of the browser used, or the settings on the computer, there could be variation in color, the resolution of the image (its sharpness), and in the positioning of the image on the screen. For some settings, participants in this experiment would have to scroll the browser window to reveal the complete image. It is hard to say how this might have affected results, but it is likely to have reduced the reliability of scoring.

A key problem is that the time for which a participant saw each of the pictures was determined by the speed of their response. The quicker a participant responded, the sooner a disgusting image would be removed. Some of the images used were quite horrible. It is possible that some participants would click a response quickly just to get rid of a distasteful image. This could have led them to give less consideration to the selection of response on some trials, and perhaps even to them just clicking the nearest response rather than the option that best reflected their emotional reaction to the image. Even worse, some participants may have developed a strategy of responding quickly to images based on a superficial feature, in order to avoid the distress of seeing upsetting pictures. For example, they might decide that as soon as human flesh is detected, they will click to prevent any more of the image from loading in the browser window. If this did happen, it would again undermine the **construct validity** of the study, because responses would derive from whatever criterion was used as the basis of the strategy. For instance, if a participant started to respond on the basis of detecting the color yellow, then responses would reflect the visibility of yellow in the images, not the level of disgust they created.

The logic of the conclusion is also questionable. Even if we were to assume that none of the methodological problems mentioned affected the findings, and that the study was valid and reliable, it is not at all clear that the results licence conclusions about an evolutionary cause for the results. That is, even if adults really are more disgusted by disease-relevant images, it does not show that this difference is caused by evolution. An alternative possibility is that the disgust reactions are learned during an individual lifetime.

A final issue is an ethical one. Participants were given little warning of the nature of the images to be used, and some were frankly distressing. For example, one showed an open wound with abscesses. Moreover, there was nothing to prevent children participating, and nothing to warn children or their parents that the images might be upsetting to youngsters. Participants were not given advice on what they should do if they felt disturbed or upset as a result of participating.

These problems relate to two important ethical issues. First, psychologists should obtain informed consent. Informed consent requires that potential participants are told as much as possible about what they may experience in the course of the study so that they can make a real choice about whether they are willing to participate. In the case of young children, informed consent should also be given by the adults responsible for the child's care.

There is an even stronger criterion that is used in medical research. This criterion is a part of the Nuremberg Principles, ethical criteria drafted in the wake of the appalling abuse of human participants by scientists during World War II. This stronger criterion requires that participants should also be told, and agree with, the aims and object-ives of the research, as well as the procedure. This principle would require the researcher to declare up front that the purpose of the study was to test a theory that the emotion of disgust had evolved as an adaptive response to disease. If this is done, the people taking part truly are participating in the research effort as co-operative partners. It is difficult to follow this principle in psychology, because of the strong possibility that knowledge of the aims of a study will influence the way participants think and behave. However, psychologists only conceal information from participants to the extent that is absolutely necessary, and reveal the aims as soon as possible. It is also consid-ered inappropriate to carry out a study if participants would be likely to be upset when they eventually discovered the research aims.

The second ethical principle raised is that researchers should protect participants from harm. To be sure, viewing the images would not cause direct physical injury. Nevertheless, certain sensitive people could be substantially upset and disturbed by the content of the images. In these circumstances, it is important to pilot test the image with representative potential participants to gauge the potential reaction, to provide adequate forewarning to participants, and to provide sensitive debriefing and follow-up support if required.

13. DOES THE SMELL OF OLD PEOPLE CHEER YOU UP?

There are some problems with the way samples of odor were col-lected, the measure of depressive mood, and with the interpretation of the results.

Donors were asked to behave in certain ways prior to and during collection of samples, but there was a lack of **objective** checking that they stuck to those rules. It could be that differences between groups were the result of differences in the degree to which they stuck to the protocol, rather than differences in body odor due to being male or female, old or young. For example, more women than men reported eating onion and garlic. Perhaps it was the tasty smell of onion and garlic that improved mood? The experimenters also reported that some were allowed a deodorant. If, say, more women than men asked for this concession, then this could be the reason for differences in the mood change. Perhaps people were happier to smell samples that were milder.

A key problem is that the effect of the home odor was actually one of the largest effects of all. The researchers did not comment on this, which is surprising. Only one of the body odors had a stronger effect than the home odor control. Black (2001) reported t-tests comparing each experimental group with the control home odor group using Chen and Haviland's data. He found that none of the differences was significant. That is, none of the body odors produced a larger decline in depression scores than the home odor. As Black pointed out, a group that stands out, in fact, is the group that smelled young adult men. This group was the only one that did not show a drop in depression scores.

Black also argued that the test used to measure depression was not an appropriate test to assess short-term changes in mood. The questions asked about the frequency of depressive feelings over a period: "How often do you feel. . . ." We should not expect answers to such questions to change quickly over a two-minute interval. In a rebuttal, Chen (2001) indicated that the test had been adapted to make it suitable as a measure of short-term changes in mood. You might like to have a look at her paper and evaluate that claim yourself.

A third issue that concerned Black was the way that the press had picked up on this study. It was publicized quite widely, and the press reports were not always balanced and careful in their presentation of the findings. The press tend to write with the aim of entertaining their readership, and it is common to find them presenting results in an exaggerated or salacious way. As Chen pointed out, researchers have only limited control over the way their research is reported by journalists. Wherever possible, investigators do accept responsibility for attempting to ensure reporting is balanced, and that their findings are not presented in a misleading way.

14. CAN POSITIVE EMOTIONS REPAIR NEGATIVE FEELINGS?

The films shown were validated in a different form to the one in which they were used here. In this study, only the first 100s of each film was shown, and the soundtrack was not used. It is unclear how this might have affected results, but we cannot depend on the original validation.

This experiment also does not exclude the possibility that the emotion conveyed by the second film simply replaced the feelings of fear initially aroused. The experimental hypothesis specifically claims that the negative emotion is repaired, but the results are consistent with the new emotion just supplanting the first.

This study only tests one negative emotion. It is therefore not possible to generalize it to other negative emotions (except speculatively). Similarly, we cannot really generalize the results beyond the specific **population** tested – female college students in the United States.

15. DO VIGNETTES HELP US TO UNDERSTAND THE EXPERIENCE OF DRUG USERS' FAMILIES?

The central considerations for this case study are reliability and validity. A great deal depends on the **subjective** stance of the person coding the **vignette**. There are differences in the number of themes each investigator identified, and what they thought the key themes were. The category "theme" does not appear to have been operationally defined with any great precision. One coder appears to have included additional information that was frankly speculative. There is no obvious basis for deciding whether the conclusions they reached were correct. Nevertheless, it could be argued that the process of reflecting on what people say about their experience can help us to identify important variables for future research. If that view is taken, the vignettes could be seen as a useful form of **exploratory research**.

16. IS THE "DRAW A FIGURE TEST" A VALID MEASURE OF SEXUAL ABUSE?

The problem with this study is that the hypothesis is retrospective. Relationships can occur in data sets by chance. If the hypothesis is based on the data, and the data are tested, there is a risk that spurious relationships will appear to be statistically significant.

Lilienfeld, Wood & Garb (2000) reviewed two other studies that had looked at the same relationship. Those studies found no statistical evidence for an association between tongues sticking out and sexual abuse. In other words, the finding does not replicate.

Whenever a pattern is discovered through exploratory research, it is important to say that it is a result of exploring data, and to be cautious in drawing firm conclusions. In this example, if the "draw a figure test" had been taken seriously as a diagnostic test for sexual abuse, the consequences would have been disastrous. Children who were not being abused could have been subjected to interventions, and children who were victims could have been overlooked. Findings from exploratory research need to be followed up with studies specifically designed to test the hypothesis.

17. DO DIFFERENT KINDS OF MATHEMATICS TEACHING CAUSE DIFFERENCES BETWEEN JAPANESE AND AMERICAN CHILDREN ON MATHEMATICS TESTS?

The first problem is that the difference in mathematical problem solving was confined to just one of the three types of creative mathematical operation. There is no account of why only problem integration and not the others should show a difference, since all three are said to be rehearsed by the qualitative problems to which American children are supposed to be exposed more frequently.

Second, no direct evidence is presented about the mathematics education of the specific samples of children involved in this study. The claim that experience is different was based on general surveys of education in the two countries. This evidence may be a reasonable guide, but it would be better to directly record the position in relation to the samples actually tested.

Third, it is not clear that the four processes defined by Mayer et al. have been characterized well. For example, what they term "planning" was operationalized by problems a little like this:

Which operations would you carry out to solve this problem?

Sandy had six cats. Two were run over by a truck, but then one of the others had four kittens. How many cats did Sandy have in the end?

It is not clear that a question like this is answered by planning. It could involve first just solving the problem, and then generating a

summary of the steps that were involved. Indeed, the reported summary of the solution might not actually follow the steps that had
been taken. For example, I might solve the problem by cancelling
two of the kittens against the two that were killed ($4 - 2 = 2$, if you
like), and adding the net increase of two ($6 + 2 = 8$). However,
I might still report a more direct: $6 - 2 = 4$; $4 + 4 = 8$. If the problems
do not really measure the planning process, then this reduces the
construct validity of the tests.

A fourth set of difficulties relates to the matching of groups of
children. Recall that students were grouped by MAT scores. This
meant that some of the highest scoring US students were matched
with rather average Japanese students in groups 2, 3, and 4.

There is a general problem with **matching** people who have
extreme scores on one variable to compare their performance on a
second variable. This is called **regression to the mean**. If the two
variables are moderately correlated, inevitably those scoring highest
on one variable will not score highest on the other. In this example,
the top US student for MAT is not likely to be also the top scoring
student on the MP test. This would tend to make the US children
in the top groups, defined by MAT scores, have a poorer standing
on the MP test. As Stigler and Miller have pointed out, however, that
would make it less likely that the US students would outperform
the Japanese children they had been matched with. Therefore, in
this instance, regression to the mean is not a viable alternative
explanation.

Nevertheless, Stigler and Miller identified other problems with
matching in this study. I will describe one of them here. As we have
noted, the very best US students, the top 5 percent, were matched
with the top 70 percent of Japanese students. The bottom 44 percent
of US students was not included in any group. The top 5 percent of
any cohort are likely to be particularly intelligent and motivated
individuals. Higher levels of intelligence and motivation could explain the better MP scores of US students in these groups, rather
than differences in exposure to certain types of problem.

The Stigler and Miller paper describes other problems with the
matching procedure used by Mayer et al. Matching is an important
methodological issue in a number of areas of psychology. For example, in the study of children with disorders such as autism, it is often
useful to compare performance to children who do not have the disorder. However, if they are simply compared to other children of the
same age, there will be many other differences than just the absence

of the specific disorder. An interesting series of articles discussing these issues appeared in the *Journal of Autism and Developmental Disorders* in 2004 (e.g. Mervis & Klein-Tasman, 2004).

18. DO MOTHERS CAUSE REFERENTIAL AND EXPRESSIVE LANGUAGE LEARNING STYLES?

The problem here is knowing whether the mother's behavior is shaping the child, or the child's language style is shaping the mother's behavior. That is, which is the cause, and which is the effect. For example, it is possible that the mother has detected and is responding to the style of language use that the child displays.

19. DO INFANTS THINK AN OBJECT THAT DISAPPEARS HAS CEASED TO EXIST?

Piaget initially made the first observations with his own children. The sharpness of these observations and the careful, systematic way he followed them up mark him as one of the greatest of scientific psychologists. The theoretical questions he posed as a result generated a great deal of research in the following years, and psychologists are still striving to fully explain these findings.

One possible alternative explanation for the 5-month-old children failing to reach for hidden objects is that they might lack the **motor skills** to do it. They may not be able to hold their posture, reach forward and lift a cloth, and then pick up an object. If the reason they do not retrieve the object is because their motor skills are too weak, then the result has little to do with cognitive development.

This possible explanation was tested in an experiment described by Bower (1982). In his experiment, he wanted to see if children would be startled when an object that had disappeared came back. If they thought it had ceased to exist, they should be surprised to see it again. He measured infants' heart rates, so that the results would not depend on them having developed motor skills of reaching and grasping. If they were startled, their heart rate would leap. The object was initially in view of the child, but then was hidden by a screen. After a short delay, the screen was removed. When the screen was removed, Bower found that infants expected the object to still be there. Their heart rate rose only if the object had disappeared. This suggests that, at some level, the infants did have an understanding that objects that go out of sight continue to exist.

20. CAN INFANTS ADD AND SUBTRACT?

Cohen & Marks (2002) argued that there are other possible explanations of Wynn's results. They noticed that in both cases, addition and subtraction, the "incorrect" final scene was actually the same as the initial scene at the start of the trial. For example, in the addition trial, the stage starts with one doll, and following addition of another, the impossible scene has the stage set with one doll again. It could be that infants look longer just because they prefer to look at something familiar. To support this possibility, Cohen and Marks cited a number of previously published studies where it was found that infants prefer the familiar.

A second possibility is that the children do not understand fully numbers and arithmetic, as Wynn (1992) suggests, but only understand that some quantities are more than others. In the addition task, for instance, they may not understand one plus one makes exactly two, they might only appreciate that adding a doll should lead to a larger quantity. If that was all they understood, it would not be a complete understanding of number and addition, but it would be enough to get the right answer on this task.

Cohen and Marks reported an experiment of their own which included a $1 + 1 = 3$ **condition**. One doll began on the stage alone, another was added, but when the screen was lowered, there were three dolls in view. Consistent with both alternative hypotheses, children spent the same time staring at the stage in this condition as they did in the $1 + 1 = 2$ condition. According to Wynn's interpretation, they should be surprised to see three on stage, and should look for longer.

Cohen and Marks included another new condition in their experiment. This condition was designed to distinguish between their alternative hypotheses (familiarity preference and understanding quantity but not number). In this condition, $1 + 1 = 0$. When the screen lowered, the stage was empty. What do the three explanations predict in this situation?

Explanation	Predicted behavior	$1 + 1 = 0$
Prefer the familiar	Look longer if final scene matches first scene	Not stare
Understand quantity only	Look longer if not a larger quantity	Stare
Understand number	Look longer if not the exactly correct answer	Stare

The resulting mean looking time for "$1 + 1 = 0$" was 6.4s. This was less time than if $1 + 1 = 2$ dolls (7.5 s) or $1 + 1 = 3$ (8.8s). This pattern is not consistent with the theory that children compute exact values, which would predict longer stares at $1 + 1 = 0$ than at $1 + 1 = 2$.

Cohen and Marks concluded that Wynn's interpretation of her results was too strong, and that a weaker explanation would suffice. Cohen and Marks were certainly correct to highlight the importance of controlling for familiarity when testing hypotheses using this experimental technique. However, not all investigators are convinced that their data refute Wynn's position. For example, Wynn has argued that Cohen and Marks' experiment was more complicated for the infants than hers, and this may have overloaded the infants. This interesting debate can be followed in a series of peer commentaries published alongside the paper by Cohen and Marks.

21. DO CHILDREN UNDER 2 YEARS OLD TRY TO INFLUENCE OTHER PEOPLE'S MINDS?

Others have argued that there is an alternative explanation (Shatz & O'Reilly, 1990). It could just be that the child was determined to achieve the material goal. The child could just have learned that adults respond to certain types of gesture by bringing desirable things close enough to get hold of. In short, the child could have a behaviorist theory of adults, rather than a cognitive one. In some cases, there was no obvious material objective. The child's goal seemed to be to gain information, for example. However, in these cases the child's aim could simply have been to keep an enjoyable interaction going. This could all happen without the child having beliefs about mother's mind.

Debate on this issue has continued in the literature. Shatz and O'Reilly conducted an **observational study** and found that children were more likely to try to clarify requests (94 percent) than statements describing the situation (84 percent), supporting their view that what underlies their behavior is the pursuit of a material objective rather than mutual understanding. Golinkoff (1993) replied that 84 percent seemed like quite a high number, and that the children's pursuit of common understanding rather than just a material objective was, in fact, demonstrated by Shatz and O'Reilly's result.

More recently, Shwe & Markman (2001) have reported an experimental study designed to assess this question. They contrasted situations in which children did not get what they wanted. In one situation, this happened because of a misunderstanding, in the other the experimenter made it clear that she had understood what the child wanted. The task involved placing two objects in front of the child, and asking which the child wanted. For example, one might be a toy ball, and the other a blue sock. The child would typically ask for the ball. The experimenter would either say "You asked for the ball. . . . Here is the sock" (no misunderstanding, just frustration) or "You asked for the sock. . . . Here is the sock" (misunderstanding). Counting gestures as well as utterances, the researchers found that children were about three times as likely to repeat the request when there had been misunderstanding. Shwe and Markman concluded that children do appreciate whether their listener has understood.

This case study illustrates the way that research questions are investigated by different researchers, using different approaches. Researchers debate each other's findings. Understanding of the question is refined over time, and more precise tests of hypotheses are formulated. At any given point in the process, different researchers may draw different conclusions. Over time, a body of evidence is gathered that tends to support one position or another.

22. CAN TALKING TO SOMEONE WHO IS LESS RACIST INFLUENCE PREJUDICE?

There are a number of difficulties with accepting this conclusion on the basis of the evidence presented in the case study. The first problem relates to the way children were allocated to high and low prejudice groups.

The procedure for dividing children into high and low prejudiced groups is not described completely explicitly. It appears that this was done separately for each of the three classes. The criterion is described as the median for "same-sex classmates." It seems likely that it was done separately for each class because the design required children to be paired with someone from their own school, and of their own sex. Consequently, there were in fact six different cut-offs for high and low prejudice. The paper does not list the actual values used as cut-offs for each group. However, it is clear that there must be at least some overlap between high and low prejudice participants across the study. That is, certain pupils would have been assigned to the high prejudice group even though their counter bias scores were in fact higher (less prejudiced) than scores for some individuals in the low prejudice group in other classes. From the description given, we cannot tell how large that overlap may have been. It is important to bear in mind, then, that the definition of high and low prejudice is relative to the local average. It could be that none of the children were actually prejudiced, compared to norms for the **population** as a whole, or in relation to some absolute standard.

A second problem is that, although the two measures used to assign children to groups correlated highly, they did not correlate perfectly. In a few cases, they were not consistent. Despite this, the experimenters managed to assign all the children to either the high or low prejudice group. This means, inevitably, that a few children were assigned to a group when only one of their scores pointed that way.

Third, the pattern of change in scores is exactly what we would expect given ordinary **regression to the mean**. Assuming that the MRA is not perfectly reliable, people will not get the same score every time they are tested. In fact, it is likely that, on average, people who get extreme scores first time around will have less extreme scores the second time they are tested. Therefore, it is to be expected that the average for the high prejudice group will indicate lower levels of prejudice, purely as a result of this effect of measurement error. The change for the group that was initially classified as having low prejudice also moves in the direction predicted by regression to the mean, although the change is not significant.

These three problems relate to the way children were allocated to groups. Another problem concerns the design. There were three experimental groups, but there was no **control group**. The changes in the experimental groups could have been a result of the conversations children had with each other. However, they could have been the result of **maturation effects** or history effects. A maturation effect is a change that occurs because of a separate process of development or learning in the participant. The children were a few weeks older at the time of the second test. They would have been a little more experienced, and perhaps their thinking skills or knowledge about race could have developed.

History effects arise when an event occurs during the study that affects participants' behavior. For example, there may have been a programme on television dealing with race that many of the children saw, perhaps a documentary or an episode of a favorite soap. Or perhaps their teachers had been picking up on the theme of race in class. This last possibility is really quite likely. I have conducted studies on children's road safety in schools, and teachers often like reassurance that their children have "done well." It is entirely possible that they might coach the children between the tests.

This does not explain why there was no decrease in prejudice scores for the low prejudice group. Note, however, that their scores were near the ceiling. That is, they scored near to the maximum possible score. Indeed, to have such a high mean, many of the 44 children in the low prejudice group must have scored the maximum both times. In short, with the low prejudice group, there was little scope for improvement. This means that the results could be explained by history or maturation.

There were one or two features of testing procedure that were perhaps not ideal. The reliability of the MRA test appears to be good. However, more than one version was used. The first, full version of the test is the one for which existing reliability measures hold good. However, it was used in both an English and a French version. Was reliability established for both versions? Translation is not a trivial matter, and a word that appears to be a literal translation may have different emotional connotations. These connotations could affect responses in a test of attitudes. In addition, the test was used in a shortened form to evaluate changes in attitude after the test. This was necessary because two items had been used in the conversation and, the experimenters reported, because they were short of testing time. Nevertheless, we may question whether the shortened form was as reliable as the full form. In fact, it is quite possible that the shorter version would have been less reliable. All things being equal, a test that has fewer items will be less reliable.

This leads us to a further problem with the task. In the task, children do not appear to have the option of refusing to allocate a property to anyone. The instructions indicate that the child should assign the attribute to one or more of the imaginary children. It is at least possible that some participants would feel that none of the imaginary children should be considered "bossy." What kind of process are children applying in such instances? The child could conceivably be thinking: "none of the children are bossy, but I must give out the cards; maybe it is better to give out one card, then fewer of the children are bad," and then handing out one card at random. In that case, the result would not reflect prejudice.

There are two detailed aspects of presentation that the study did not control with precision. The first is the time gap between the first MRA test and the second session. This varied between 3 and 5 weeks. It is possible that the length of the lag affected results. Possibly those who were re-tested sooner gave more similar responses. In addition, there was no precise control over the difference in MRA score between children in each pair. Within the high and low prejudice groups, there was a lot of variation. A child at the top of the low prejudice range could be paired with a child at the bottom of the high prejudice range, leaving only a small gap between them. Equally, children could be paired who were at opposite poles of the scoring range. This lack of precise control would tend to reduce the power of the experiment, making it harder to detect effects. It also has the potential to lead to accidental **confounding** of these variables with the groups. It is just possible that, for instance, there was on average a shorter delay for high prejudiced children, and in that case length of delay would be confounded with level of prejudice.

It is also the case that the experimenter testing the children's MRA score following the conversation would not have been **blind** to the child's classification as high or low prejudice, and would have been aware of the hypothesis that the conversation would lower prejudice. In the MRA test, each item is handed to the child separately by the experimenter, who repeats the standard question orally. It is conceivable that the experimenter unwittingly biased the child's responses.

The experimenters used the counter-bias measure because this measure had been found to be a useful and reliable measure in previous research. That is a good reason to use a measure. However, we can ask why the counter-bias measure should turn out to be a better measure than a more direct measure of bias. Recall that the counter-bias score totals the negative properties given to Whites and the positive ones given to Blacks. It would also be possible to total the negative properties given to Blacks and Chinese. However, this possible measure is not reported in the paper.

It is always sensible to consider how well the results of a study could be expected to generalize. In this case, participants were all White, likely middle-class, children, growing up in an environment that we can guess was relatively homogenous racially. The results could be different for other kinds of children.

23. DO 4-YEAR-OLD CHILDREN BELIEVE A PERSON'S RACE CANNOT CHANGE AS THE PERSON GROWS INTO AN ADULT?

This is a very strong conclusion to draw from the study described. There are a number of alternative explanations, some of which Hirschfeld identified in his papers.

One possibility is that when children were asked about growth, they simply judged which child looked overall most similar to the adult. Hirschfeld addressed this in his experiment by testing another group, who were asked to judge which child was most similar to the target. The fact that children showed a different pattern of responding when asked about similarity does suggest that the judgements about growth and inheritance were not simply based on judging which of the two children was overall most similar to the target person. This is a nice example of the way the design of an experiment can anticipate and address potential alternative explanations.

A second possibility raised by Hirschfeld is that when children were asked about growth, for some reason they made a special or focused similarity judgement, using the narrow criterion of skin color as the sole test of similarity. Hirschfeld carried out an extra study to test this. In this supplementary study, participants had to choose whether a black or white car was the target's car. The cars could also have large or small dimensions. None of the age groups showed a greater preference to pick the same color car over one that matched for size.

Hirschfeld took this as evidence that the children were not using a narrow color criterion in the main study. However, this supplementary evidence does not completely rule out the possibility that children were using color similarity to make the judgement about growth, because it could be they apply different criteria when making judgements about relationships between living things than they apply to artifacts like cars. It is also conceivable that the narrow basis of a similarity judgement of one of the other racial features, such as hair. The supplementary study does not rule that out.

There is, however, no direct evidence that children's responses were mediated by a concept of race. They could, for example, have noticed, item by item, that there were several points of match between the physical appearance of the target adult and one of the children. The child with the same "racial" appearance had similar hair, facial features, and skin color. The older children may simply believe that these individual features are inherited. There is no direct evidence that they considered the features as a cluster, a corporeal concept of race.

Hirschfeld's conclusion that children believe race is immutable is also not directly tested. The task only requires children to indicate a preference in a situation where they must choose one thing or the other, for example either racial appearance or occupation. The results show that, given this choice, children tend to match on racial appearance rather than body build or occupation. But this shows only that children think it is less likely racial appearance will not match, it doesn't show that they believe it is immutable, that it cannot change.

Hirschfeld's studies have raised many interesting questions, and the interpretation of his results has been debated by other researchers (Kim, 1997; Hirschfeld, 1997). If you are interested in this topic, you may enjoy reading those articles.

24. CAN PERSONALITY PREDICT WHO WILL HAVE A DRIVING ACCIDENT?

There are a number of difficulties with this conclusion. First, as Trimpop and Kirkcaldy acknowledged, the crucial variable of accident involvement is based on self-report. It is possible that certain types of personality make people more likely to understate their accident history, and this could obscure the interpretation of the data. Ideally, there would be an independent and **objective** measure of the number of accidents each participant had experienced. One possible source of such data would be insurance company records.

It is also unclear from the original paper what kind of incident was counted as a driving accident. Accidents could involve widely varying levels of seriousness. Was a small scratch to paintwork made while parking counted as equivalent to a high-speed crash involving other vehicles? Related to this, no distinction was made between accidents in which the driver was to blame and accidents in which he was not at fault. If another driver motors into the rear of your car while you are waiting at a stop light, that is unlikely to be caused by your personality. If risk-taking makes drivers more likely to have accidents, it will be easier to detect this relationship if the study focuses on accidents in which the driver was at fault. Including accidents that were caused by another road user will cloud the picture.

The average period for which participants had been driving was 5.2 years. However, the range of driving experience varied greatly. The youngest, aged just 16, the minimum age for a driving licence in Canada at the time of the study, could have had their licence for no more than a few months, while some of the older drivers would have had their licence for many years. Drivers were compared on the basis of the number of accidents across their entire driving career. However, this means treating as equal two drivers with the same number accidents even if they had been driving for very different lengths of time. A driver who has, say, one accident in 10 years is surely less of a risk than someone who has had one accident in a year. It would be better to have taken driving experience into account. One way to do this would be to use the number of accidents per year, or per 1,000 km driven, as the variable.

In relation to the personality measures, the original paper does not directly report figures for **reliability** and **validity**. It does provide references to the sources of the questionnaires, and so the interested reader can follow this up if they wish. However, a firm evaluation of the study depends on a consideration of the reliability and validity of these measures, and ideally some information on this would be reported. It is common for researchers to report on the reliability and validity of questionnaires in the method section of a paper.

25. DO VIOLENT VIDEO GAMES MAKE PEOPLE AGGRESSIVE?

These results do not provide evidence for a causal relationship from playing violent videogames to violent behavior. It could easily be that more aggressive children are drawn to playing video games, rather than game-playing causing aggression. Moreover, the result only held for one measure of aggression, and only for boys, once television viewing and school performance were taken into account. There were no relationships between home video game playing and aggression. Dominick's paper emphasized that the relationships he observed between video game playing and aggression were relatively weak, and that the relationship with school performance was much stronger.

As Dominick noted, many of the measures used rely on **self-report**, and it is always possible that different groups of children differ in the reliability of their self-reports. For example, it could be that children who say they do well at school are more likely to underreport acts of violence. These may simply be children who want to present themselves in a positive light. Conversely, there may be children who want to play the role of tough guy. They may overstate how much time they spend hanging out at the arcade, and how often they engage in violent acts. Self-report measures are vulnerable to effects like this **impression management**, and cannot be regarded as perfectly valid. Ideally, we would make independent and **objective** measures of variables like school performance, television viewing, and so on.

A final problem is that the study does not differentiate violent and non-violent video games. Children were asked how long they spent at the video arcade, but they may have spent most of their time playing non-violent video games. This lack of precision in the measure will tend to make it less sensitive, and therefore make it harder to detect any relationship with aggression that might exist.

One thing that is very nice about this study is the way that it partly replicates the earlier study by McLeod, Atkin & Chaffee (1970). This allows some direct comparisons to be made between the two pieces of research.

26. CAN PLAYING ACTION VIDEO GAMES IMPROVE YOUR ATTENTION SKILLS?

As described so far, this study has what is called a **quasi-experimental** design. Participants were not randomly assigned to be players or non-players. Rather, the experimenters have used existing groups of people who either play or not. This prevents us from concluding that video game playing causes the better attention skills. That is because any other difference there might be between the groups could be the reason for the different attention skills scores. It could be that people who have better attention skills in the first place were drawn to video game playing, and that game experience did not improve those skills. Conversely, people with poor attention skills might try the games, find they do not do well, and then give up. By either of these two mechanisms, visual attention skills could determine whether people play video games a lot, rather than the other way around.

What is terrific about Green and Bavelier's paper is that they realized this. They ran a fifth experiment to test for a causal relationship. For this experiment, they randomly assigned participants to a game play condition and a **control condition**. All participants were first given **baseline** tests of visual attention, including the useful field of view test. They then played video games one hour a day for 10 days. Those in the game play group played an action video game, while the control group played Tetris. Tetris requires visuo-motor coordination but, according to the authors, is less demanding in terms of processing several objects at once. After 10 days, they were tested again, and the action game group showed greater improvement of attention skills. Green and Bavelier also found that the extent of improvement in attention skills was moderately correlated with the extent that they improved their score on the action game. This correlation is additional evidence that it is the game playing that improves attention skill.

It is worth making the point that the control condition was nicely constructed. It did not consist of just doing nothing. It was very similar to the experimental action game condition. The only difference was the critical difference: the action game loaded players with multiple events, and Tetris did not do this so much. Another nice feature of this study was that it employed the useful field of view task. This task was originally developed to help identify drivers with a high risk of crashing, and has been shown to discriminate between older drivers with good and bad accident records (Ball et al., 1993). It is possible that action video game playing may help develop skills that are important in everyday life.

This study was a wonderful combination of different research methods, quasi-experiments and experimental designs, to reach conclusions with high internal and external validity.

27. CAN PEOPLE SCAN A SCENE MORE EFFICIENTLY BY IGNORING THE LOCATIONS OF OBJECTS THEY HAVE ALREADY EXAMINED?

One alternative explanation, considered by the researchers, is that the visual system uses the positions of the first set of green distractors as a clue to the locations where the target could possibly appear, since the blue letters can only appear in the spaces left between the green letters. From this theory, Watson and Humphreys generated the following hypothesis: If the green Hs help because their position identifies possible locations for the target, then green blocks of the same overall size should work equally well. Moreover, because the blocks don't share the same shape as the target, unlike the green Hs, it should be even easier to search for the target than in the normal simple search condition.

Watson and Humphreys (1997) ran an experiment to test this hypothesis. Green blocks, the same size as letters, appeared first, in the locations usually occupied by green Hs. After a 1,000 ms delay, the blue letters appeared. Participants also performed the simple search condition with just blue letters, and no preview with green blocks or letters. The results showed that responses were on average slightly faster in the simple search condition than with green blocks. Watson and Humphreys concluded that the gap effect was not likely to be the result of the clue to possible target location that the preview of distractors could provide.

It is an outstanding feature of the paper by Watson and Humphreys that they not only considered this alternative explanation for their results, but also designed and ran a new experiment to test the alternative hypothesis. Moreover, Watson and Humphreys considered and carefully tested several other possible explanations. Their paper is a good example of the careful development of a theoretical position by excluding, one by one, possible alternative explanations.

This successive elimination of alternatives is typical of the very best experimental research. It is less easily accomplished with applied or field research. One criticism often made of laboratory research is that it describes only laboratory behavior, and the results do not carry over to the real world. Sometimes, that may be true. In this case, the results may be relevant to a wide range of everyday behaviors. For example, when a pedestrian crosses a road, she checks for approaching traffic. Many pedestrians who are struck by cars say they did not see the car at all, until it hit them. Aspects of visual attention are likely to be relevant to understanding why this is.

28. DOES WORD FREQUENCY MAINLY AFFECT THE EFFICIENCY OF PROCESSING AFTER THE WORD HAS BEEN IDENTIFIED?

Balota and Chumbley's argument has been challenged by other researchers for a number of reasons (Monsell, Doyle & Haggard, 1989).

1.   They did not match the phonological structure of high and low frequency words. The phonological structure of a word is the pattern of sounds that form the word. It could have been that the high frequency words had sound patterns that were easier to say aloud. If frequency and ease of pronunciation were confounded in this way, it could explain the effect in both the no delay and delayed conditions.

2.   The target word was still visible when the cue to say it aloud appeared. It could be that participants triggered the word identification process only when the signal to respond appeared. For example, a participant might see the word "bee," identify it, start thinking about bees, honey, summer days, and then, when the signal appeared, look back at the word on the screen and re-start the reading process. If that is what they did, then word identification processes could cause the frequency effect.

Against this interpretation, at even longer delays, like 1,400 ms, there was only a very small effect of frequency. If anything, we might expect participants to be more likely to re-start processing at longer delays.

The researchers making these criticisms went on to carry out some interesting experiments to test their alternative explanations of Balota and Chumbley's results. In one, they re-designed the task to maximize advance preparation. For example, the target word was removed from the screen before the signal to avoid the possibility that participants might re-start the reading process only when they received the "go" signal. In addition, the delay was always the same, and so was predictable, and participants were given three attempts at each word. This maximized the opportunity for them to complete identification and poise themselves to respond as soon as the signal appeared. For the second and third attempts, there was no frequency effect. From this experiment, Monsell et al. concluded that frequency effects in lexical naming do not arise mainly from processes, such as articulation of the response, occurring after the word has been identified.

29. DO THE FIRST AND LAST LETTERS OF A WORD PROVIDE SPECIAL INFORMATION THAT HELPS A READER PERCEIVE THE WORD?

This piece of research is a nice example of taking a hypothesis from theories that have been advanced in the research literature, and designing an experimental test of the hypothesis. As often happens, however, there follows debate about whether the experiment provided a good test, and about the correct interpretation of the results. This case study illustrates the way researchers debate such issues.

A paper by Jordan, Thomas, Patching & Scott-Brown (2003) argued that there were some problems with Briihl and Inhoff's study. These researchers were intrigued by Briihl and Inhoff's results, because their own earlier studies, using single words as stimuli rather than lines of text, had suggested that the first and last letter pair does play a special role in reading. Jordan et al. pointed out that Briihl and Inhoff's experiment only tests the role of different forms of preview in parafoveal processing, the interval just before the target was fixated, during which only the critical letter pair was visible in the prime. They argued that even if the first and last letter pair played no special role in this part of processing, they could still be specially important in other, later, stages of the overall reading process.

Briihl and Inhoff's study had deliberately chosen to focus on parafoveal processing, and it is a good feature of their study that they focused so precisely on a specific aspect. However, it remains possible that the first and last letter pair play a key role at other points. Jordan et al. argued that it was especially unlikely that the last letter could play a role during parafoveal processing, because it would be furthest from the fixation point, and so would be seen less well due to the reduced **acuity** further from the fovea. Indeed, this point had been made by Briihl & Inhoff (1995).

Jordan et al. questioned the technique of substituting xs for letters. When xs are substituted, information is not only lost about the identity of the individual letters, but information is also lost about the overall shape of the word. For example, the first letter of the word "tin" is tall, whereas the first letter of the word "can" is not, and this difference affects the overall shape of the word. Perhaps, they argued, when letters are substituted with xs, it is the loss of information about overall word shape that makes a difference.

Jordan et al. also pointed out that there is an additional difference between the conditions, beyond the intended **manipulation**. The manipulation varied which positions were available in the prime. However, it also varied how many transitions there were from a dummy letter x to a real letter. When the first two letters are available, there is one transition, between the second and third letters. For example, "bu [transition] xxxxx." However, in the first and last letter condition there are two transitions, one after the first letter, and one just before the last letter. For example, "b [transition] xxxxx [transition] o." It could be, they argued, that the occurrence of two of these unusual transitions rather than one was the variable that affected gaze duration, and not the difference in letter position. The difference between letter positions was confounded with the number of transitions. Although they had no specific evidence that these alterations in shape would influence reading, Jordan et al. argued that it would be better to be cautious and try to allow for the possible effects.

An additional statistical quibble is that Briihl and Inhoff did not report a direct comparison between the initial letter or exterior letter pair conditions and the no preview condition. Although the statistics they reported show that these conditions were worse than full preview, and not different to one another, no statistical confirmation was provided that they were better than no preview. (This contrast was reported for the body condition.) If they were not different from a no preview condition, rather than concluding that the advantage of partial parafoveal preview was largely due to the initial letter, it would have been more accurate to conclude that partial preview was not of assistance, or that the method had not been sensitive enough to detect its assistance.

Jordan et al. designed a new study to look at the role of the first and last letter pair in foveal as well as parafoveal reading. They faded and blurred letters in the words, and these degraded stimuli were presented throughout the viewing period, both during parafoveal and foveal processing. By degrading letter pairs, rather than substituting with xs, the overall word shapes were preserved. Passages

were presented with about one word in ten degraded, and the
dependent variable was the time taken to read the whole passage,
of about 500 words. By measuring overall reading time for the passage, Jordan et al. allowed all aspects of the reading process to be
involved. However, this is at the expense of being precise about where
in the reading process any effect occurs. They found that degrading
letters slowed reading, but they found that it was degrading the first
and last letter pair that slowed reading the most, slowing reading by
about 25 words per minute.

The debate about the appropriate interpretation of the results of
these studies continues. For more detailed information on the experiments, and to follow the discussion, see the papers cited already, and
the further commentary in Inhoff, Radach, Eiter & Skelly (2003)
and Jordan, Thomas & Patching (2003).

30. HOW DO PEOPLE UNDERSTAND AMBIGUOUS WORDS?

The proponents of the re-ordered access model responded to Martin
et al., and have pointed out two main difficulties with their conclusion (Rayner, Binder & Duffy, 1999).

The first concerns the selection of items. It is not clear that the
individual items were accurately classified into dominant and subordinate meanings. Rayner et al. compared Martin et al.'s classification to a classification based on data they had gathered locally, and
noticed a number of discrepancies. For example, Martin et al. gave
"screen over a door to keep out insects" as the dominant meaning of
screen, but in Rayner et al.'s norms it was "cinema screen." Rayner
et al. found 24 of the 56 original items were problematic in this or
similar ways. They ran two experiments without those problematic
items, one using self-paced reading times, the other using eye movements to measure reading time. In both there was a subordinate bias
effect even in strong contexts.

The second issue concerned the predictions Martin et al. had made
from the re-ordered access model. Recall that according to this model
context can boost the subordinate meaning if it is contextually
appropriate. However, the model does not set the amount of the boost.
It could be just enough to run the subordinate meaning alongside
the dominant meaning, in which case we would see delay selecting a

meaning, the subordinate bias effect. But it could be a stronger boost, enough to run the subordinate meaning into a strong lead. In that event, the model would not predict any extra delay, no subordinate bias effect. In short, Rayner et al. argued that their model was consistent with elimination of the subordinate bias effect. They did concede that previous explanations of their model in their earlier papers might have made that unclear.

This controversy raises a general issue. One reason for confusion about the predictions of the re-ordered access model was the lack of precision in the original specification of the model. If a model is not expressed precisely, different people can interpret it in different ways. This is one reason why many experimental psychologists and cognitive scientists prefer models to be specified explicitly and precisely as mathematical or computational models.

31. DID WATCHING A PLAY IMPROVE ATTITUDES TOWARDS SPEEDING?

The researchers carefully arranged a **control group**, and made sure that the control group took the same attitude questionnaires so that their scores could be compared to the children who had seen the play about safety. However, there are other differences between the two groups that could have affected the results. First, the control group members were not involved in any activity other than the attitude assessment. It could be that simple participation in a safety-related activity was enough to improve attitudes for the first group, and that the specific content of the play was not what determined the outcome. In trials like this, it is best to arrange that the control group activity differs as little as possible. For example, the control group might have been shown conventional information films instead of the play.

The second difference was that the two groups went to different schools. As a result, we cannot be certain that it was not some difference between the schools that caused the different outcome. For example, perhaps the school where children saw the play had also participated in other safety training during the two-week interval before completing the second questionnaire. Ideally, the experimenters would randomly assign participants to their groups. We could then assume that the only systematic difference between the groups was the experimental treatment. Studies in which groups are not assigned randomly are termed **quasi-experiments**.

Another general difficulty with this type of research is that just attitudes are measured, and not driving behavior. This is only a valid approach if the measured attitudes correlate with behavior. Only then can we be confident that the intervention would make a contribution to safer driving.

32. DOES DDAT TREATMENT WORK?

This case study looks at an evaluation of an intervention that was reported in the journal *Dyslexia* in 2003 (Reynolds et al., 2003). Immediately after the article appeared, a number of researchers in the field raised methodological problems, and published discussions of those problems in the same journal. You may find it interesting to read some of those discussion papers.

Here are some of the main points:

- The details of the DDAT procedure are a commercial secret, which makes it almost impossible for anyone to replicate the findings independently.
- The control group did nothing. This means that the difference between the two groups was not just that the experimental group received DDAT, but that the experimental group received a treatment intervention of any sort, along with all the attention and concern that goes with that, whereas the control group received nothing. This raises the possibility of a **placebo effect**. The control group should have received some other activity that provided similar amounts of contact, attention, and so forth.
- There were important differences between the groups before the study started. They were not well matched on NFER scores, and seven members of the experimental group, but only five members of the control group, were receiving additional help with reading at school, outwith the DDAT program. Results could be attributable to these differences rather than DDAT.
- Many of the children did not appear to have serious reading difficulties in the first place. Some dyslexia screening test scores were better even than the threshold for being judged "at mild risk," and some children's reading ages were in advance of their chronological age (see ranges in Table 32.1). If there was

not a problem in the first place, why would one expect DDAT, or any treatment, to fix it?
- There is obviously concern about the independence of the study given that the commercial organization had initiated the research. The psychologists involved are well known and have good track records: there is no reason to doubt their good faith. But the existence of a commercial interest associated with the outcome of a piece of research will always lead some people who read the study to qualify their interpretation of results that suit the commercial interest.

In reply, the original authors of the study have said that they nevertheless felt the study contributed to the field as a first step in addressing questions about the utility of DDAT. They said that it was difficult to design the perfect study because resources to carry out the study were limited.

33. CAN IT BE ETHICAL TO EAT YOUR PARTICIPANTS?

The animals were treated well during the study. Ethical codes for psychologists are published by national organizations. The codes require animals to be looked after carefully, to be treated humanely, and for harm to be minimized. They also require that no harm be suffered unless it is justified by the scientific and practical benefits of the study. However, these codes do recognize that the lives of animals are sometimes terminated.

In the original paper, the authors pointed out that it was normal for a proportion of lambs to be removed from their mothers at this research station. This was done to avoid problems such as the mother having insufficient milk, particularly when she had given birth to more than one lamb. Against this, we could note that the lambs used were twins who were both taken from their mother. This appears to go further than the normal treatment of lambs in this facility. The motivation for removing the lambs in this case was clearly the desire to carry out the study reported. In addition, we might argue that just because a certain pattern has become normal, that does not guarantee that it is ethical.

Nevertheless, it is normal practice in many countries, such as France, to farm sheep for meat. Apart from the initial separation from their mother, and the occasional brief tests lasting a few minutes, the treatment of the lambs in this study was similar to the treatment of other lambs at the facility. The researchers pointed out in their paper that, in fact, the lambs' welfare could be monitored better in their experimental groups of six, and, as it turned out, they had no more problems with health than other lambs not involved in this experiment. In the end, some of the lambs were slaughtered for meat, but there is no suggestion that their fate was affected by participation in this study. People do eat lamb.

Another consideration is whether the results of the project might be used to benefit other sheep in the future. Research like this could be used to influence the way livestock is managed to reduce stress experienced by animals. If so, then it could be argued that distress experienced by the lambs in the course of the study can be counterbalanced by benefits to other sheep. This would be a type of utilitarian argument, in which the overall benefits of a course of action are weighed.

Whether there can be such a benefit crucially depends on the validity and soundness of the research carried out. For that reason, it is important to evaluate the methods carefully. This consideration should also apply to research with human participants. Their time and comfort should not be dissipated in badly designed studies that could not yield worthwhile information.

In this instance, there are some possible criticisms of methodology that I will just make briefly. First, all the lambs were of the same breed and were a similar age. This would tend to make them quite similar in appearance to begin with, and would tend to reduce the magnitude of effects when comparing twins of penmates with complete strangers. Second, it is not clear from the report whether the person recording the number of bleats was **blind** to the hypothesis. This is not likely to be a major problem, because the measures were relatively well defined and operationalized in objective terms. Nevertheless, the ideal would be that the person scoring trials would be unaware of the research hypothesis, and unaware which condition they were scoring, to avoid unwitting bias.

34. THE BURT AFFAIR

Burt assumed that the environments in which the two twins were brought up would be uncorrelated. However, there is every reason to expect that they would be related. Adoption agencies tend to have criteria for placements that reduce the range of possibilities. It is quite likely that there would have been some similarity in the environments in which the twins were brought up.

There is also a problem with the statistics. The correlation coefficients calculated for the two samples are exactly the same, although the number of twins has increased. It is most unlikely that the correlations should be exactly the same, and this coincidence indicates that some error may have been made. Indeed, it has been suggested that Burt may have fabricated these figures.

Burt's papers give the impression that he gathered additional twin data as late as the 1950s or the 1960s. However, it appears unlikely that this was the case. For example, one researcher who he appears to have claimed collected new data up to 1955 apparently moved to Dublin in 1950. A possible explanation is that he mislaid some data, perhaps because of wartime disruptions, that had first been gathered much earlier. Unfortunately, one of his colleagues arranged for the destruction of his original records a few days after he died.

Those who support him point out that the correlations he reported were actually quite close to those subsequently found by other researchers. However, it has also been pointed out that, in other studies, Burt did not detect what has become known as the Flynn effect. According to Burt's data, average intelligence scores in London did not rise significantly over a period of decades. More recent research by Flynn (1987) strongly suggests that a measurable rise would have been expected. Few psychologists now believe that the figures reported by Burt can be relied upon. At the very least, he ought to have been more explicit and straightforward in reporting the sources of his data.

35. DO PEOPLE FROM NORTHERN ENGLAND HAVE LOWER IQS THAN PEOPLE FROM SOUTHERN ENGLAND?

Although these data indicate that IQ is to some degree inherited (father–son correlations), it does not show that the differences between the north and south are inherited. It could be that environmental differences explain the difference in average IQ between the areas. For example, those in the south may have had better access to schooling, they may have enjoyed better nutrition, may, on average, have been less affected by illness, and so on.

This case study is unusual in that it is fictional. However, I have included it because it illustrates a common misunderstanding about the logic of evidence regarding the inheritance of traits. The example shows that something more is required to make a case that some difference between groups is genetically determined. Clearing up this possible source of confusion should help make it easier to think about Case 37.

36. THE FLYNN EFFECT: IS EACH GENERATION MORE INTELLIGENT THAN THE LAST?

An alternative explanation is that younger people have more familiarity with the kinds of test that are used. Even though they are not helped by learning factual information, increased experience with toys like the Rubik's cube, and the use of abstract reasoning tasks in television game shows could increase their familiarity with such tests. This would give them an advantage in formal IQ tests.

It could be, however, that socioeconomic advances may have made a real contribution, particularly in developed countries, since the war period (when in many countries food was rationed and schooling was disrupted, for example). Average height has also increased. Flynn's analyses suggest that the gains are too large to be explained by this alone.

This is an open question. The evidence gathered by Flynn is not sufficient to allow a definitive conclusion, and the issue is being debated (Neisser, 1998).

37. DO RACE DIFFERENCES IN IQ IMPLY THAT IMMIGRATION TO THE UNITED STATES WILL LEAD TO MORE SOCIAL PROBLEMS?

This publication has been one of the most widely discussed and debated pieces of social studies research in recent times. Many commentaries have been written, some praising the work, some criticizing it in strong terms (Jacoby & Glauber, 1995). The commentaries in Jacoby and Glauber, and elsewhere, make a number of critical points not mentioned here, and you will find it rewarding and enjoyable to read both those commentaries and the original book by Herrnstein and Murray. I focus on some methodological issues that call into question the quality of Herrnstein and Murray's empirical work. However, I will also consider issues relating to the quality and appropriateness of their presentation, and the connections they made with politics.

The test of cognitive ability used was out of date. It was included in the NLSY so that it could be re-normed. Herrnstein and Murray do not explain whether the "IQ" scores they reported were based on the 1940s norms, or revised norms. Moreover, the AFQT was not intended for use with 14-year-olds. These problems raise doubts about the reliability and validity of those assessments.

The NLSY samples only one generation. This means that all conclusions need to be qualified because results could be influenced by cohort and period effects. These effects usually arise when differences between groups can be attributed to special features of the particular time when those people were a given age. For example, if the relationship between cognitive ability and economic success is affected by the economic cycle, then these results would not apply generally. It could be that during a recession or a period of low economic growth, there is a strong relationship between cognitive ability and economic success. Even if that were so, it would remain possible that during periods of higher economic growth the correlation does not hold, or is weaker. The design of the study prevents the authors from excluding this alternative hypothesis.

In any case, data from the survey were only available for the first 11 years, to 1990. An alternative hypothesis to the conclusion that people with a lower IQ do not attain high standards, is that they take more time to get there. Because the study looks at such a brief window of lifespan development, it cannot exclude this alternative explanation. The youngest participants would only have been 25 years old when the last measures were gathered.

The description of the survey sample in the text of the book is brief, and it does not, for example, indicate the relationships between Age and the other variables studied. It is possible that, for instance, the average age was lower for those with lower cognitive ability scores, or for those in certain ethnic groups. If that were the case, then these variables would be to some degree confounded with Age. The presentation of information about the sample is not as detailed as it would be in a journal article, and that prevents us from fully assessing the methodological adequacy of the study. Appendix 3 of the book indicates that Age was included in the statistical analyses, but that does not adequately address the problem.

In Table 37.1, I presented some data from the book showing the percentage of children with serious behavioral problems for mothers in each cognitive class. Table 37.1 is repeated here for convenience. It is difficult to understand how all but one of the groups could have more than 10 percent of their children in the bottom 10 percent. Only group 2, the "Bright", have less than 10 percent. Moreover, there is very little difference in the percentages reported for the top four groups, and certainly no clear correlation between AFQT group and incidence of behavioral problems across those groups. The authors attempted to explain away the 11 percent figure for the top group as sampling error, which is possible, but a relatively weak explanation for data that would otherwise tend to contradict their conclusions.

Table 37.1. Behavioral problems and maternal AFQT score.

Mother's AFQT "class"	Percentage of children with worst behavior problems
1	11%
2	6%
3	10%
4	12%
5	21%

Note: Data from Herrnstein & Murray (1994, p. 227).

Herrnstein and Murray treat the Flynn effect in a peculiar way, as if it was a separate phenomenon from the effects of immigration on US national IQ. The Flynn effect is a description of changes in measured IQ incorporating all influences, including the effects of migration and economic change. There is no such thing as "The Flynn effect separate from migration," that policy makers can take for granted as an upward influence on future average national IQ.

As a number of commentators have pointed out, it is important to consider **effect size** as well as the significance of relationships. In many instances, although there is a significant relationship between

IQ and some outcome, the relationship is not large, and IQ certainly does not account for most of the variation. We can be sure that many other factors than IQ are related to poverty, crime, and marital breakdown. The design of the study does not in fact permit us to draw the conclusion that IQ is a cause of these outcomes. This is a correlational study, which can demonstrate an association, but not a casual link.

There are aspects of the rhetorical style that detract from the scholarly tone of the work. I give two examples. For some analyses, participants were grouped according to "cognitive class." This could be just a convenient way to present data, but the labels for the groups, and the very term "cognitive class," are loaded. They represent beliefs about the interpretation of the data, rather than the data itself. The authors appear to see a world stratified into groups suited for different purposes. The AFQT was not designed to reliably differentiate five intellectual "classes." There is also some inconsistency between the early reassurance that ". . . it should make no practical difference in how individuals deal with each other," and the ultimate conclusion that public policies need to be changed so that people are treated in a different way to the way they are treated now. The initial reassurance gives an impression of balance and fair-mindedness, but in the end they actually do draw strong conclusions about actions that should be taken. It would have been more straightforward to have consistently indicated that they believed there were implications for the way people are treated.

Psychologists do need to be careful when offering prescriptions for public policy. If the immigration policy in the United States were changed, then it would have large implications for very many people, not just migrants, but also for people currently living there. For example, if, in fact, the future economic, social, and intellectual prosperity of America stands to be enriched by migration, then excessive restriction could damage the country. Psychology as a science is ill equipped to forecast the effects of policies like these. The hypotheses are not amenable to experimental test. Herrnstein and Murray's study does not have a sufficiently rigorous methodology to allow even relatively weak conclusions to be drawn. Psychologists should clearly distinguish between science and opinion, between what can be shown to be the case and what they speculate might be so. Indeed, one of the authors, Murray, was not actually a professional psychologist. The conclusions about immigration policy go beyond the science of psychology, and cross into the territory of **politics**.

38. IS SEXUAL REORIENTATION THERAPY EFFECTIVE?

Spitzer himself was aware that methodological problems with this study preclude any strong and direct conclusion that sexual orientation therapy can change sexual orientation. In particular, he noted that there was no control group. For evidence that the changes were caused by the therapy, we would need to compare the results with a group who were similar in every respect except for the **intervention**. Without this **control group**, we cannot rule out the possibility that the change is due to changes in the individuals caused by the mere passage of time, or events linked to the passage of time. For example, it could be that family pressure to have children occurred over time, and this is what drove changes in these individuals.

The second important thing to note about this study is that the participants were a highly select sample. When designing a study to draw causal conclusions, our ideal is to randomly assign participants to the control and experimental groups. In this case, participants were recruited after the fact. Spitzer, in responding to criticism of the study on this point said that carrying out a prospective study would have meant a long wait for results, and this retrospective method was at least a useful way of getting some quick information. However, there were particular characteristics of the participants that may have biased the results.

Some participants were recommended for the study by their therapists. The therapists who practice such therapy would, presumably, have been likely to recommend clients representing successful outcomes. Indeed, the criteria for participation included the condition that no one could participate unless they believed they had benefited from the therapy. This inevitably biases the outcome. A related problem is that because the sample is biased, those for whom the therapy was not a success are not represented in the sample. Consequently, we cannot estimate the proportion of clients treated who saw a benefit. It could be that, in a representative sample, those reporting a benefit would be in a very small minority. It is possible that 98 percent of the time, the therapy does not work, and the 200 recruited represent the lucky 2 percent who feel the therapy was beneficial. Spitzer acknowledged this problem, but argued that his aim had been simply to demonstrate that the therapy could at least sometimes produce positive outcomes.

The sample was drawn in part from organizations who support such therapies on the basis that homosexuality is morally wrong. Most participants had strong religious convictions that might reinforce the view that homosexuality is morally aberrant. Around 80 percent of participants had publicly advocated the therapy before taking part in the study. There is a real possibility that participants would have given the kinds of answers that would be consistent with these beliefs. Because the data were based entirely on self-report, and the questions were relatively transparent, the study has little protection against this possibility. Participants could have modified their answers to manage the impression that they gave.

A problem with the method of measuring outcomes is that it relied on participants being able to remember detailed information about their sexual behavior and feelings not only for the last 12 months, but also for the 12-month period prior to the start of therapy. We cannot work it out exactly from the information given in the paper, but it looks like the year before therapy was typically 12 years before the date of testing. It is difficult to be confident that memories from so long ago would be perfectly accurate.

It is unfortunate, too, that Spitzer himself conducted the interviews. Ideally, the researcher gathering data would be **blind** to the research hypothesis. Spitzer did have a researcher check his coding of responses in a subset of the interviews. Coding is the translation of responses into the categories being used as a measurement. So, for example, say someone is asked "On a scale of 0–10, how satisfying have you found heterosexual sex in the last 12 months?" If they answer "8," the correct coding for this study is "8." In this study, coding was transparent, and would not be expected to be biased. Coding was simply a matter of correctly recording responses. **Experimenter effects** would be a greater problem for the way the questions were asked, particularly in an oral interview. The experimenter might unwittingly hint at the most desirable response by modulating their intonation or giving some other paralinguistic cue.

A serious problem lies in the claim, made by Spitzer, that his study shows that reorientation therapy does not cause harm. It appears that the study evaluated harm only with one, relatively superficial question about depression. Other possible types of harm were not evaluated at all, and the question about depression merely asked for a self-report for the before and after periods. This is hardly likely to be a valid and reliable measure. Like all the questions, it could have been affected by participants' desire to appear to be virtuous and successful examples. Furthermore, as we have noted, the failures were excluded from participating at all.

There is another major problem with interpreting this study. The central **construct**, reorientation therapy, is not well defined. By this I mean there is no coherent and consistent definition of what constitutes reorientation therapy. A wide range of different approaches is counted, with only the aim of changing sexual orientation being a common feature. Not all approaches that were included even involved a therapist. Why would one expect such a diverse range of approaches to have similar effects? From a study like this, it is impossible to work out which ingredients of reorientation therapy were relevant to bringing about changes in orientation.

When this study was published in 2003, several researchers published commentaries alongside the article. Some argued that the paper should not have been published at all because it was so methodologically flawed. Commentators also raised ethical issues in relation to publication of the report. A report supporting reorientation therapy, they argued, would support homophobic attitudes in society. In addition, the uncritical claim that reorientation therapy does not cause harm might lead people to have misplaced confidence in such activity. Against these considerations, Spitzer argued that people who wished to be helped to change sexual orientation should be provided with the opportunity for therapy as long as there was some evidence that it could work. This, he contended, was consistent with their right to make informed choices.

39. CAN A MEDIUM CONTACT THE DEAD?

The ratings by the sitters are potentially biased because they believe in life after death, and their **subjective ratings** determine the accuracy ratings for the professional mediums. The subjectivity of the sitter also is used to fill in the details of the medium's reading, which is vague enough that it could find a match in many people's lives. In contrast, the control subjects have to find the detail for themselves, a somewhat trickier task. The **control condition** does not, therefore, provide an adequate basis for comparison.

There is also no independent verification of the sitter's assessment of the reading. No-one checks that there really was an aunt Millie.

40. DOES ALCOHOL MAKE PEOPLE OF THE OPPOSITE SEX LOOK PRETTIER?

The first issue is that this study had a quasi-experimental design. Participants are not assigned to the alcohol and no-alcohol groups by the experimenter, they had assigned themselves. Therefore, any difference in the ratings they gave to faces could be due to other systematic differences between the groups. For example, perhaps the drinkers were, on average, more lonely. The loneliness led them to drink, and the loneliness led them to rate opposite sex faces more highly. That is a possible alternative explanation for the results. Alternatively, the two groups could have come to the bar for different reasons. Perhaps the drinkers had come out to party, the non-drinkers just to meet friends. This difference in motivation might have affected attractiveness ratings. There is any number of possible differences between the groups other than the difference in alcohol consumption. If participants had been randomly assigned instead, then we could assume that, on average, in the long run, there would be only random differences between the groups on irrelevant variables like loneliness.

One possible problem with a randomized experiment is that it would raise additional ethical issues. In such an experiment, participants would be given alcohol that they might not otherwise have taken. We know that alcohol is a harmful drug. It heightens the risk of accidents, and can cause lasting damage to health. The **quasi-experiment** has the advantage that it takes data from people who have themselves chosen to drink. The results of the quasi-experiment at least indicate that alcohol might lead to a difference in attractiveness ratings. This preliminary evidence could be used to indicate that there is a realistic possibility that a true experiment would produce a positive result. This would help justify running a subsequent randomized controlled trial.

A second weakness is the reliance on self-report. It is not unknown for young people to brag about drinking prowess. Perhaps some people overstated their alcohol consumption, perhaps others claimed they had not been drinking when, in fact, they had. It would be better to directly estimate blood alcohol level. A related problem is that there was quite large variation in the amount of alcohol the drinkers had taken. A person who had one small glass of wine three hours ago may be relatively sober, yet they would have been placed in the same group as someone who drank six in the last 30 minutes. In a controlled experiment, the researcher would provide carefully measured drinks, so that the amount of alcohol taken could be known with certainty. This lack of control over alcohol levels would have reduced the power of the experiment, and made it harder to detect any effect due to alcohol.

Third, it is worth asking whether the study designed could have distinguished the facial attractiveness hypothesis from the others. Could the results not be equally well explained by the alcohol expectancy hypothesis, for instance? If the drinkers believed that people find opposite sex faces more attractive after drinking, then this could have become a self-fulfilling prophecy, producing the results obtained.

41. DO INEXPERIENCED FOOTBALL PLAYERS PERFORM COGNITIVE TASKS BETTER WHEN THEY ARE TIRED?

There are several problems with drawing this conclusion on the basis of the study as reported.

First, it is not clear that the cognitive task was a reliable and valid measure. Details of the assessment of **reliability** and **validity** are not given. Second, it appears that the same sequence of slides was shown six times to each participant. If that is so, participants would have grown familiar with the items, and may have responded in later sessions simply by repeating their earlier answers. Alternatively, they may have mulled over the items between sessions, changing their responses. Either way, participants may have been using a strategy tailored to the experimental situation, and this casts doubt on the validity of the cognitive function test.

Third, if the same test of ability is repeated, participants will almost always improve just because they have practised the specific skills involved in taking that particular test. This, rather than fatigue, could explain why scores improved at half-time in session two.

Fourth, presentation of the cognitive function test would have taken 15 minutes. There were 45 slides, each shown for 20s. Within a few minutes, good athletes like these would have substantially recovered from fatigue. Consequently, the tests at half-time and full-time would not be pure assessments of task performance in conditions of fatigue.

Fifth, the error rates were really rather high, 40–50 percent across conditions. Recall that two of the options were "don't know" and "another alternative not shown." Someone guessing the answers would probably avoid those two. That suggests that a guessing strategy alone could give you an error rate as low as 67 percent. This casts doubt on the **validity** and **generalizability** of the cognitive task. If even college players performed near the floor on this task, what was it measuring?

In the end, it is not clear that the experimental procedures assessed cognitive function in conditions of fatigue. The measures of cognitive function were not very general, and possibly not valid. Moreover, they participants may not have been physically fatigued throughout the period in which the test was completed.

42. ARE DECISIONS ABOUT PENALTY KICKS INFLUENCED BY EARLIER DECISIONS THE REFEREE HAS MADE?

A first problem is that **experimenter effects** could have occurred. The experimenter pauses the video and asks the participant to make a decision. It is possible that experimenters unwittingly influenced responses. It appears from the paper that the experimenter was not **blind** to the condition during testing. The experiment could instead have been automated, so that no-one interacted with participants during testing, or a researcher who was blind to the research hypothesis and the condition being tested could have been employed.

Three other criticisms were raised in a commentary by Mascerehas, Collins & Mortimer (2002). They argued, first, that the viewing angle in a video is different from the normal viewing angle for a referee, who sees the game from ground level. They said this could explain why only 18 percent of the participants gave the same decision as the original referee. This criticism does identify a potential problem with the **ecological validity** of the study. Possibly the findings would not generalize to real refereeing decisions. However, Mascerehas et al. were mistaken to say only 18 percent made the same decision as the original referee. In fact, 82 percent made the same decision for the first incident, and a third of these also made the same decision for the second.

Second, Mascerehas et al. questioned the use of both players and referees as participants, suggesting that only qualified referees should have been used. However Plesner and Betch found no significant differences between players and referees. It is therefore not clear how using only referees as participants would have changed the outcome.

Third, Mascerehas et al. argued that the data do not specifically support the conclusion that people give different decisions to the two incidents because they were balancing things out. All the evidence shows is an association between successive decisions. It is certainly correct that the study does not show a causal link and, indeed, Plessner and Betsch carefully avoided claiming that it did. Mascerehas suggested an interesting alternative explanation. Perhaps participants awarded the second penalty to avoid an escalation of foul play in the match. A referee may let the first incident pass to keep the game flowing, but if fouls begin to become more frequent, the referee may award a penalty to set an example and signal to players that they should behave better. This is an interesting hypothesis, but it does not explain the cases in which participants awarded only the first penalty.

43. IS SUSIE MORE LIKELY TO MOVE TO SUSSEX THAN DURHAM?

Pelham, Mirenberg & Jones (2002) actually reported 10 different studies in the same paper, all tending to support this same conclusion. An interesting commentary by Gallucci (2003) drew attention to some problems that concerned the statistical analysis in particular.

First, notice that the pattern does not hold perfectly for every connection between a particular place and name. For example, actually more Georges moved to Virginia (71 percent) than Georgia (69 percent), and there are more Virgils in Kentucky (7.6 percent) than Virginia (2.6 percent).

Second, look at the relationship between the observed and expected numbers of people with a matching name for each state. This information is presented again in Table 43.3. The expected frequency is the number predicted if there is no difference in the distribution of names across states. The hypothesis derived from the theory of implicit egotism is that the observed number will be higher than expected in each of these cases.

Table 43.3. Relationship between observed and expected frequencies for four names.

State/Name	Observed	Expected
Georgia/George	3,592	3,520
Kentucky/Kenneth	526	518
Louisiana/Louis	699	476
Virginia/Virgil	198	309

From the data in Table 43.3, it is clear that the observed frequency is not much different to the expected frequency for Georgia and Kentucky. For Louisiana, there is a large excess of men called Louis, but for Virgina, there are far fewer Virgils than expected. That is, it looks like two states probably show no effect, one state shows an effect in favor of the hypothesis, and one state shows an effect counter to the hypothesis. We would have to check this using significance tests, and that, indeed, is what Galluci did. Across Pelham et al.'s studies he found this kind of pattern. When you looked at individual links, the hypothesis did not hold up consistently.

The excess of men called Louis in Louisiana remains as a possible piece of evidence in favor of the theory, but there are two possible alternative explanations. First, it could just be chance. Just by chance, there will be an uneven distribution of names. If you make enough comparisons, even if there is no real effect, some will be statistically significant. That is the nature of statistical inference: the 5 percent level is the level you would only expect 5 percent of the time if nothing but chance sampling differences were determining the results. But equally often some will be significant in the opposite direction, and that is what we see in this case. The other alternative explanation is the ethnic explanation. Maybe there are more people with ancestral connections to the French-speaking world in Louisiana, and maybe that helps explain why the name Louis is more common there.

A third problem is that when the researchers focused just on the men who were most likely to have moved, rather than having lived in the state all their lives, the **effect size** dropped. Why? This should be a less noisy test of the hypothesis. The reduction in effect size implies that actually a large part of any association between people's names and the places they live is due to something other than implicit egotism.

Finally, Gallucci pointed out that the statistical analysis is based on totals derived from just the four names being tested. Of course there are very many other first names. The percentage of people called George in Georgia is much less then 69 percent. This affects the statistical analysis because the expected frequency for George will depend heavily on which other three names are selected to be included in the study. If we used Vincent instead of Virgil, for instance, that would alter the total number of people recorded in the table, and would therefore affect the outcome of the analysis.

44. ARE PEOPLE MORE HOSTILE TOWARDS IMMIGRANTS BECAUSE THEY PERCEIVE THEIR PRESENCE AS A THREAT?

Florack, Piontkowski, Rohmann, Balzer & Perzig (2003) found that people who reported higher levels of perceived threat were less likely to support integration of immigrants, and were more likely to express support for assimilation, segregation and expulsion. The hypothesis suggested that the higher levels of perceived threat brought about these different attitudes. However, there are several qualifications that have to be made to the interpretation of these findings, most of which were noted by the original authors.

First, the study was not a true experiment because participants were not randomly assigned to have different levels of perceived threat. This makes it impossible to draw any conclusion about a causal relationship between perceived threat and attitudes towards acculturation. For example, it could well be that people who have the belief that immigrants should be expelled or segregated come to believe that these people pose a threat, perhaps because having this belief, or just expressing it to others, helps them to justify their support for expulsion or segregation.

A second difficulty lies in the selection of the sample of participants, which is unrepresentative of German society in general in two ways. Almost all the participants were men, and the participants were people attending Chamber of Commerce and Trade occupational training courses. This makes it difficult to generalize the results beyond men working in small and medium-sized enterprises, businesses that were more likely to send men than women for occupational training. Of course, the views of such people are important and worth understanding, but we have to be careful not to assume that the findings would apply to other types of people.

The third group of problems relates to the quality of the measures used. Although **reliability** values were reported, they were relatively modest for the measures of attitudes towards types of acculturation, which were based on a small number of items. More importantly, there is no direct evidence relating to **validity**. For example, we do not know whether participants interpreted the questions in the way that the researchers intended. Some questions were actually worded using the technical labels for the theoretical **constructs** the researchers wanted to measure. For instance, the word "threat" was used in the rating scale for the measurement of perceived threat. We have to bear in mind, then, that what the questionnaires were measuring depended on the participants' understanding of the terms used in the items. Finally, the basis for the measurements was self-report. Consequently, the responses can only reflect attitudes to the extent that participants have explicit conscious access to them. In addition, the participants could have shaped their responses with a view to **impression management**. That is, they could have moderated their replies so that the answers gave what they felt would be an appropriate impression.

The researchers addressed many of these issues in a second study in the same paper. In the second study they manipulated the level of perceived threat by getting participants to read newspaper articles that portrayed immigrants in different ways. After reading the articles, they gave their ratings. Participants were college students, and were randomly allocated to read articles that portrayed immigrants positively, as a threat, or gave a neutral portrayal. This study found that participants who read negative articles were less likely to accept the integration of Turkish people into German society. This finding is interesting, and comes closer to supporting the case that perceived threat causes a lower acceptance of integration. It is a virtue of this paper that the researchers recognized that they could not draw a causal conclusion from the first study, and attempted to run a follow-up experiment to test the hypothesis more directly. In addition, using college students helps broaden the range of participants. Moreover, the findings, if correct, would have important implications for society in general. For example, it would suggest that by altering the editorial policy of newspapers we could affect people's attitudes towards immigrants. However, it is possible that participants in this experiment could have recognized the experimenter's hypothesis, and responded to perceived demand. It also would be a little surprising if reading a small number of newspaper articles could bring about significant changes in attitudes that would have formed over a number of years.

4

RECAP

I hope that you have enjoyed reading the case studies, and that the solutions have helped you to think critically about research in psychology. I want to just briefly pull together some of the ideas.

A research paper begins with a research question. The research question is chosen because it has a bearing on some theoretical or applied concern, and is expressed as a hypothesis. The more precise the theory, the easier it is for experimenters to draw out a specific, testable hypothesis.

In the process of translating the research question into a specific hypothesis, the researcher has to identify a task or procedure that can tap the psychological constructs that form the basis for the theoretical explanation. For example, if a researcher thinks attention skills are important, the researcher will need to select a way of measuring attention skills. This step involves operationalizing the construct, identifying a behavior or some other response that carries information about the construct. To the extent that the measurements do correspond to the construct, they possess construct validity.

For psychology, operationalizing constructs is a difficult step. We cannot see and touch our constructs, the way a chef can see, touch, and even taste the ingredients of a recipe. We are not even absolutely certain that any given construct exists. We just expect that they do, because they help us make sense of things, because our theories use these constructs in explaining behavior. And we become more confident that they exist because we seem to be able to measure them. For example, some psychologists believe there is a personality dimension extroversion, others believe there is a stage in development called the sensorimotor stage, and others believe in a thing called working memory. These are all constructs. The instruments we use to measure them, questionnaires and experimental tasks, operationalize those constructs, and open up a window on the mind.

Psychological instruments vary in reliability. Some produce consistent measurements from one week to the next, others produce very different results in the hands of different researchers. They vary, too, in validity, but it is difficult for us to assess validity directly because we cannot ever directly measure the underlying construct. An argument for the validity of an instrument can be built up by assessing the correspondence between the measures it produces and the real world. If an instrument correlates well with other measures of the same thing, then it will be considered valid.

Psychologists are interested in people. But people vary a lot, and people are intelligent and adaptable. It is important for any research study to take this into account. Researchers take care in the selection of participants, because it is easy to end up with a biased or unrepresentative sample. Researchers try to plan their procedure to avoid subject or experimenter effects that could distort behavior. Researchers also try to make sure their tasks have ecological validity, so that participants are not using different strategies and forms of behavior to those they would ordinarily use. This is important so that researchers can have confidence their results will generalize beyond the testing situation to the real world.

Most aspects of behavior can be influenced by a range of factors. For example, the time it takes someone to name a word will be affected by the word's frequency, concreteness, length, whether it is threat related, the time of day, and so on. Typically, a research hypothesis is concerned with only one or two explanatory variables. Experimenters therefore need to find ways of preventing the other influential variables from distorting results. In the worst case, an interesting explanatory variable ends up confounded with an irrelevant variable, and it is impossible to discern which is responsible for the results. To avoid problems such as this, researchers use controls. Controls allow experimenters to exclude alternative explanations for the results.

Once a study has been completed, the researcher has to interpret the results. The interpretation of statistics does require care, even if nowadays, thankfully, the calculation is done for us by computers. Both effect size and statistical significance are relevant to deciding whether a result is important. In judging statistical significance, it is necessary to take into account whether test assumptions were met, whether the study was exploratory, how sensitive and reliable the instruments were, and how large the sample was. Then, in drawing conclusions from the results, we must bear in mind the nature of the study. In particular, it is only really possible to draw conclusions about a causal relationship between a construct and some behavior when the study was a true experiment. Quasi-experimental and correlational designs leave open alternative explanations. Nevertheless, exploratory, correlational, and quasi-experimental research can play an important role in a research program. They can build the foundations for experimental research, and they can help narrow the range of possible explanations when experimental research is not practicable.

Researchers need to communicate their findings carefully. It can create serious difficulties for interpretation if aspects of the procedure or the data are unclear or potentially misleading. Fellow researchers are unable to properly evaluate the work if the report is vague. Of course, findings are debated. Researchers argue about the merits of each others' work, and these debates propel the psychological sciences forward. They raise new questions, and motivate new research. I have tried to give a flavor of that research process in the case studies.

CROSS-REFERENCE CHART

This chart lists key issues that were discussed in the case studies, and indicates which case studies involved different issues. Terms are explained in the glossary.

Issues	Case studies illustrating the issues
Formulation of the research question	30; 37; 40
Design	
Confounding and controls	2; 5; 13; 22; 28–29; 31–32; 38; 40
Experimenter effects	8; 11; 22; 38; 42
History and maturation effects	22; 31
Cohort effects	2; 37
Cross-sectional studies	2; 36; 37
Causality	11–12; 25–26; 37
The participants	
Sampling	7; 10–12; 22; 32; 38
Matching	17; 32
Attrition	10
Cohort effects	2; 37
Impression management	2; 9; 38
Acquiescence	7
Measurement	
Construct validity	11–14; 17; 22–24; 31; 38; 41
Self-report data	2; 7; 8; 24–25; 38; 40

Issues	Case studies illustrating the issues
Retrospective reports	2; 8–10; 24–25; 38
Subjective ratings	4; 15; 39
Secondary sources	7; 9; 17
Interpretation of materials	4; 7; 11–12
Selection of materials	6; 12; 14; 30
Ceiling effect	22
Other reliability and validity issues	12; 22; 24; 37
Internet research	12
Quality of reporting method or data	22; 32; 34; 37
Statistical issues	
Hypothesis testing	2; 4; 13; 16; 29
Multiplicity	43
Effect size	5; 25; 37; 38
Regression to the mean	17; 22
Interpretation	
Alternative interpretation of findings	1–3; 10; 12–14; 19–21; 23; 27–28; 34–37; 40
Weak explanation of anomalies	7; 10; 17
Speculative reasoning	9; 15
Generalizability	14; 22; 26–27; 41
Ethical and professional issues	4; 12–13; 16; 32–34; 37–38; 40
The research process and debated findings	1; 10; 15–16; 19–21; 23; 25–29; 37–38; 42–43

GLOSSARY

Accuracy How close a measurement is to the true value.

Acquiescence The disposition to agree.

Acuity Ability to make fine discriminations. Most often applied to the capacity of the visual system to discriminate fine detail.

Age effect An effect that can be attributed to the age of participants per se.

Alternate forms Different versions of a test containing different items, but designed to measure the same construct and to have similar reliability and validity. Also called *Parallel forms*.

Anecdotal evidence Evidence in the form of examples of events that have been observed. Anecdotal evidence is considered weak evidence because it has not been gathered systematically, and the examples can be chosen selectively to support any particular view. It can also be difficult to verify or replicate anecdotal evidence.

Anomaly An unusual result that is either inconsistent with other data or inconsistent with theoretical expectations.

Arousal Mental energy; alertness.

Artifact Something created or made. This term is commonly used to describe effects that are the unintended outcome of the way a study was carried out.

Attrition The loss of participants in a study in which testing continues over a period of time. Some researchers call this mortality.

Baseline An initial measure made before a study begins, to which data gathered during the study are compared.

Before-and-after study A piece of research that compares data obtained before some event, typically an intervention, with data on the same variables after the event.

Biased sampling A sampling process that creates an unintended systematic difference in the sample. For example, if the first 20 volunteers are assigned to condition A, and the next 20 to condition B, there is a systematic difference between A and B because A contains the earlier, more eager volunteers.

Blind   A researcher is blind when he or she does not know the experimental hypothesis or does not know which condition each participant is in when testing is carried out. See also *Double-blind.*

Bonferroni adjustment   A numerical adjustment to the critical value of an inferential statistic, designed to allow for the effect of multiple testing. The critical value is adjusted in direct proportion to the number of tests being made.

Broadly similar results   This phrase indicates that the analysis of data using a different method led to similar conclusions about which effects were significant, and similar sizes of effect.

Carryover effect   An effect on participant responses that is caused by the participant having already participated in another part of the study. For example, participants may learn some information in an early condition that helps them in later conditions.

Cohort effect   An effect that is due to the time at which a person was born. People who were born at a given time have many things in common, because they lived through the same period. For example, men born before 1960 in the United Kingdom are likely to have experienced corporal punishment at school, whereas men born after 1980 are much less likely to have enjoyed that discipline. Cohort effects are confounded with Age effects in cross-sectional studies, because the older people have a different age to the younger people, but were also born at a different time.

Co-morbidity   The occurrence of two illnesses or pathologies at the same time in a single case. For example, co-morbidity of depression and anxiety occurs when someone has both conditions.

Condition   A component of a study in which a particular combination of settings for the independent variables is experienced by participants.

Confirmatory analysis   Statistical analysis that tests a hypothesis.

Confounding   Two variables are confounded when they vary together so that their effects cannot be distinguished. For example, imagine a researcher wants to compare the personalities of swimmers and football players, to see whether swimmers are less extroverted. The researcher goes to test the swimmers in the morning after their dawn training session, and the football players just before their evening practice. This method would confound (at least) two variables with the independent variable sport. First, it confounds time of day with choice of sport. Perhaps everyone has lower scores for extroversion before breakfast. Second, it confounds fatigue with choice of sport, because one group is tested after training, the other before. There is no way to tell whether differences between the groups are differences between swimmers and footballers, between people early in the day and late, or between people who are tired or fresh.

Consecutive sample   A sample formed by recruiting a consecutive sequence of everyone who appears in a certain period. This method of sampling is frequently used in medical research. For example, someone interested in the causes of road accidents might recruit all the drivers who come to hospital for treatment in a given period.

Construct   A variable or mechanism postulated by a psychological theory.

Construct validity   The extent to which a measurement procedure correctly measures a construct.

Control condition   A condition included to provide a comparison with experimental conditions in which independent variables are manipulated. For example, imagine an experimenter wants to know whether people are quicker to identify words if they see a target word with a related meaning just before it. The experimenter would compare performance in that condition to a control condition in which an unrelated word comes before the target.

Control group   An additional group of subjects who are assessed but who do not experience the experimental manipulation. For example, a researcher who wants to evaluate the effectiveness of an intervention might also recruit a group of participants who do not receive the intervention, for comparison. The measurements of the control group are intended to show the effect of irrelevant aspects of the procedure, such as the sheer boost from meeting such a charismatic researcher. Any extra improvement in the experimental group can then be attributed to the intervention itself.

Control variable   A variable that is measured or held constant to avoid its effect from confusing the interpretation of the results.

Convenience sample   A sample gathered composed of participants who were relatively easy to recruit, rather then being formed systematically. Sometimes called *Opportunity sample*.

Convergent validity   Correspondence with other tests supposed to measure the same thing. See also *Divergent validity*.

Correlation statistic   A statistic that quantifies the relationship between two variables.

Correlational design   A study that examines whether variables are associated.

Counterbalance   To arrange the conditions of a within-subjects study so that order effects are eliminated.

Criterion validity   The degree to which the scores produced by a measurement correspond to some criterion variable in the real world. For example, the criterion validity of personnel selection tests can be assessed by comparing the test scores to a measure of job performance.

Cross-sectional research   A study in which groups are formed and assessed at a single time. For example, a study of cognitive development that sampled children of different ages would have a cross-sectional design. The children in each age group would be different. In contrast, a longitudinal design follows a particular group over time, so that the same children are tested at each age. See also *Longitudinal research*.

Cross-validation   Checking that a result holds good with different subsets of the sample.

Demand effect   An effect caused by participants' beliefs about what they are expected to do.

Dependent variable   A variable whose value depends on variation in the independent variables. Alternatively, the variable whose value is predicted by the hypothesis.

Design   The arrangement of an individual study into conditions.

Diathesis   An attribute that leads to the development of a condition such as illness.

Divergent validity   The absence of correspondence with other tests supposed to measure different things. For example, a test intended as a pure measure of disgust would be expected to not correlate highly with a pure measure of extroversion.

Double-blind   When neither the researcher nor participants know the experimental hypothesis or the condition each participant is in when testing is carried out.

Ecological validity   The extent of relevant correspondence between the circumstances of a study and the real world situations the researcher is trying to understand. Ecological validity is high if the important aspects of the real world situation are present in the experimental situation, and if no aspects of the experimental situation distort behavior or the strategies participants use. When ecological validity is high, the results of the study will generalize to the real world, and the conclusions drawn will apply there.

Effect size   A quantitative measure of the size of an effect. Can be expressed as a difference due to the effect in standard deviations, or as a correlation.

Experimenter effect   A change in the behavior of participants caused by the experimenter rather than explanatory variables. Such effects are likely if the experimenter knows the research hypothesis, knows which condition a participant is in, and interacts with the participant. To avoid experimenter effects, it is useful to automate data gathering or to keep the person gathering data blind to the hypothesis and experimental conditions.

Experimenter error   A mistake made by the experimenter that leads to the loss of data. For example, the experimenter might give the wrong instructions, or present conditions in the wrong order, or fail to turn on recording equipment. . . .

Explanatory variable   A variable that is used to model or explain variation in a dependent variable. Similar concept to *independent variable*, except that the notion of an independent variable applies most clearly when its values are actively manipulated by an experimenter. See also *Predictor variable*.

Exploratory research   Research not carried out to test a specific hypothesis.

Fatigue effect   Tiredness, boredom or inattention brought about by participation in a study. If a fatigue effect is created, it may influence behavior in parts of the study that are presented later.

Generalizability   The extent to which results can be applied to people other than the sample tested, in situations different to the research situation. See also *Ecological validity*.

Hawthorne effect   A change in the behavior of participants caused by the fact that they are participating in a study, or are experiencing an intervention. Sometimes called reactivity. See also *Experimenter effect* and *Placebo effect*.

History effects   History effects are caused by an event that has occurred during a study but was not part of the study. For example, a longitudinal study of the relationship between extroversion and alcohol use could be affected if a war occurred and many participants were drafted to fight in the war. The experience of war could affect patterns of alcohol use. History effects can be produced by more banal events too. For example, if a researcher was comparing French language learning in groups of children at two schools using different teaching methods, the study would be affected if one school but not the other took the pupils on a trip to France midway through the study. The trip to France would be confounded with the independent variable of teaching method. See also *Maturation effect*.

Hypnotic state   An altered state of consciousness in which the subject is suggestible. Said to be similar to aspects of sleep.

Hypothesis   A statement in the form of a relationship between the values of a dependent variable in prescribed circumstances, that has been derived from a theory. For example, if I have the theory that my cat comes to the door because it hears me, I can derive the hypothesis that, in the circumstance that the cat is made deaf, it will no longer meet me at the door.

Importance   The extent to which a result matters because of its theoretical or practical significance. The phrase clinical significance is sometimes used with a similar meaning. See *Significance*.

Impression management   Control by participants over their responses in order to convey a particular impression. Often, participants will want to appear to be good, and impression management would lead them, for instance, to under-report past criminal activity. However, in some circumstances, people try to convey the impression that they are worse off than they are. For instance, they may try to convince an interviewer that they suffer from a stress disorder to claim compensation. Impression management is easier when test items or experimental tasks have a transparent relationship to the construct being measured.

Independent variable A variable whose values are manipulated directly by the experimenter.

Infant A young child less than about 1 year old, who has not yet begun to speak.

Inferential statistic A statistic that can be related to a distribution showing how likely the statistic would be to have a given value if the independent variable had no real effect. The distribution gives the probability of getting such a value, and so can be used to assess statistical significance. Because of this, the statistic can be used to test hypotheses, allowing an inference to be made about the research question.

In-group A group that someone identifies with. See *Out-group*.

Instrument Anything used to measure behavior or a psychological construct, but typically used to refer to questionnaires developed to measure psychological variables.

Internal consistency A type of reliability that can be measured quantitatively. Internal consistency is high when the items on a test agree.

Internal validity The extent to which the method used in a study permits a valid conclusion to be drawn.

Intervention An event that is introduced to a situation by an investigator to change behavior.

Lexical item A lexical item is a word.

Longitudinal research A research project that follows the same participants over a period. See also *Cross-sectional research*.

Manipulation A manipulation occurs when an experimenter changes something. The difference between the conditions of an experiment is often described as a manipulation.

Matching A method of forming samples that aims to create samples with the same average value on some variable. For example, a study comparing autistic children to learning disabled children might try to match the groups on language comprehension ability.

Maturation effect A maturation effect is caused by changes in participants during the course of a longitudinal study. For example, imagine a researcher is following a group of young men and young women over a number of years to compare how their level of alcohol use changed over time. At the age of 23, the researcher finds that women but not men start to reduce drinking. This could be due to a sex difference: being female leads you to reduce drinking earlier. However, if, for instance, more of the women had begun to get married and have children at 23, the real explanation could be that marriage and family responsibility is what causes the reduction in drinking. That would be a maturation effect. If the researcher was aiming for a clear cut test of sex differences, there would be a problem because sex difference would be confounded with marital status. See also *History effect*.

Motor skills Skills involved in physical movement.

Multiplicity   A statistical problem that occurs when a large number of inferential statistics are calculated in one study. If 100 are calculated, 5 would be "significant" even if there were no real effects. See section 1. *Evidence in psychology.*

Objective   Independent of any particular point of view.

Observational study   A research project in which the researchers watch and record behavior, but try not to manipulate or influence it. See *Participant observation.*

Operational definition   A precise and concrete working definition of a concept. For example, a researcher could say that scores on a particular ability test will be the operational definition of intelligence for the purpose of a study.

Operationalize   To convert a psychological construct into a concrete and measurable form. For instance, IQ tests operationalize intelligence.

Opportunity sample   A sample gathered by recruiting the people who happen to be available. Also called a *Convenience sample.*

Order effects   Effects resulting from the order in which conditions occur in a within-subjects design. See *Carryover effects, Fatigue effect, Practice effect,* and *Counterbalancing.*

Outcome   The result. The dependent variable is sometimes called the outcome variable because it takes a value as the outcome of the influence of predictor variables.

Out-group   A group that is not included in a group that someone identifies with. See *In-group.*

Parallel forms   Different versions of a test containing different items, but designed to measure the same construct and to have similar reliability and validity. Same as *Alternate forms.*

Participant   Someone who takes part in a research study.

Participant observation   Observation by a researcher who assumes the role of a member of the group being studied. Those being observed do not normally realize that they are participants.

Pathology   Disease or illness. The study of the causes and course of illness is also called pathology.

Pilot study   A study carried out to check aspects of procedure, to determine the appropriate levels of independent variables, or to assess which independent variables to use.

Placebo condition   A control condition in which participants are given something that appears to be the intervention being tested, but is not.

Placebo effect   The benefit produced by treatment that in fact has no direct causal relationship with the desired outcome.

Planned contrast   A statistical test making a specific comparison between groups or conditions that was planned when the study was designed.

Politics   The process of public decision making.

Population   The group an experimenter wishes to say his result holds true for. The sample is normally a subset of the population.

Practice effect   An effect on performance resulting from experience with a procedure or task.

Predictor variable   A variable whose value is believed to be associated with the values of the dependent or outcome variable. Scores on predictor variables can be used to model or predict outcomes. For example, height could be used as a predictor variable for shoe size, since taller people tend to have bigger feet.

Projective test   A test designed to draw out attitudes, dispositions or experiences that are not consciously available indirectly by charting their influence in the responses a subject gives to a stimulus or task. For example, in an ink blot test, participants say what they can see. The test assumes that the process of interpreting the blot will draw on unconscious thoughts.

Pseudo-random   A process for assigning participants to conditions, or for determining an order, that is based on some method for making an even distribution, but is not truly random.

Quasi-experiment   A study in which participants are not randomly assigned to levels of an independent variable.

Random   A process is random when its outcome depends on nothing other than chance.

Random assignment   Assignment to groups or conditions based solely on chance. This is usually constrained so that, for example, the same number of participants is assigned to each group.

Random sample   A sample formed on the basis that every member of the population has an equal chance of being selected.

Regression analysis   A statistical technique to allow the relationship between predictor variables and an outcome to be assessed quantitatively.

Regression to the mean   A statistical phenomenon that means participants who have extreme scores when first tested are more likely to have less extreme scores if they are tested again.

Reliability and validity   See section 1. *Evidence in psychology.*

Replication   A repetition of a study using the same method.

Response bias   A disposition to respond in a particular way irrespective of the particular circumstances of a trial.

Response rate   The percentage of people approached to participate in a study who agreed to participate.

Rhetoric   The manner in which information is communicated.

Sample   A set of participants recruited to take part in research. The term sample also refers technically to the data gathered from participants.

Scale   An instrument for assessing a psychological construct quantitatively. Typically refers to measures of ability or personality.

Secondary data   Data not directly gathered by the researcher.

Secondary source   A source of a description of research that is not the original research report. Review articles and textbooks are secondary sources.

Selection bias   A sampling process that creates an unintended systematic difference in the sample. For example, if the first 20 volunteers are assigned to condition A, and the next 20 to condition B, there is a systematic difference between A and B because A contains the earlier more eager volunteers.

Self-report data   Data obtained by asking participants to disclose information about themselves.

Self-selection   Participants themselves determine who will participate, or who will participate in which condition of a study. This is a possible source of bias. For example, if a researcher wants to compare two conditions, A and B, but lets participants choose which to do, the researcher will not be able to tell whether any observed difference in scores is a difference between A and B, or reflects a difference between the kinds of people who would volunteer to do A rather than B, or B rather than A.

Semi-structured interview   An interview that follows a plan, but which allows space for variation in the course of discussion from one interview to another.

Significance   In everyday language, significance can mean importance, but this usage should be avoided in formal writing because of the risk of confusion with statistical significance. A result can be statistically significant without being important. For example, there could be a significant difference in the effectiveness of two sedatives, even if the difference was tiny and irrelevant to patient care. The phrase clinical significance is sometimes used to refer to findings that have important implications for practice.

Socioeconomic status   A classification of people into social classes. There are different ways of making the classification, but they are usually based on income and occupation.

Statistical significance   A result is statistically significant when an inferential statistic is calculated that is unlikely to have been so large if the data were not influenced by the independent variable(s) being tested. The criterion is based on probabilities, and typically a result is deemed significant if it would be expected no more than 5 percent of the time if there was no real effect of the independent variable.

Stratified random sample   A sample that is selected to represent relevant groups in the population proportionately. For example, if the population contains 30 percent young men, 17 percent old men, 31 percent young women, and 22 percent old women, the stratified random sample would contain the same percentages of old and young, men and women, randomly drawn from the population. Stratified samples are intended to be representative of the population to facilitate generalization of the results.

Structured interview   An interview that closely follows a plan.

Subject   A person or animal taking part in a research study.

Subject effects   Responses of participants that arise from their participation in the study per se, rather than the conditions manipulated by the researcher. These responses are often driven by the participant's perception of what they are expected to do.

Subjective   Given from the point of view of one person.

Subjective ratings   (a) Ratings of participants or participants' behavior that involve a subjective judgement made by a researcher. For example, if a researcher rates whether someone acts aggressively, the researcher is making a subjective rating. It is usual to have a second person rate the behavior to at least check that the ratings are consistent (reliable). (b) Ratings given by participants that express their own view, especially ratings of their own experience.

Survey   A study that gathers data by asking people questions.

Test-retest reliability   A measure of the consistency of test scores when participants are given the test on more than one occasion. If test reliability is high, participants should achieve similar scores on each occasion.

Theory   A coherent system of ideas whose aim is to explain something.

Third variable   A variable that could cause change to an outcome variable, but which is not the variable considered by the researcher. For example, a researcher might discover a positive correlation between IQ and income, but this does not prove that high IQ causes high income because a third variable, such as educational achievement, that is associated with IQ, could be the direct cause of differences in income.

Trait   An attribute. In psychology, the term trait is normally used to refer to an aspect of personality.

Treatment   Another word for a condition in a study.

Twin study   A research study that compares people who are twins. Twin studies are often used to investigate the extent to which traits are inherited.

Validity   Correspondence with reality.

Values   The things a person considers good and important are values.

Variable   A quantity that can change.

Verbal report   A response from a participant that takes the form of a spoken utterance.

Vignette   A concise summary of a case.

Volunteer   A person who offers or agrees to participate without reward.

Within-subjects design   A study in which participants take part in more than one condition.

REFERENCES

Aboud, F. E., & Doyle, A. B. (1996). Does talk of race foster prejudice or tolerance in children? *Canadian Journal of Behavioural Science*, 28, 161–170.

Adorno, T. W., Frenkel-Brunswick, E., Levinson, D. J., & Sanford, R. N. (1950). *The authoritarian personality*. New York: Harper & Row.

American Psychiatric Association (1999). Commission on psychotherapy by psychiatrists (COPP): Position statement on therapies focused on attempts to change sexual orientation (Reparative or conversion therapies). *American Journal of Psychiatry*, 156, 1131.

Ball, K., Owsley, C., Sloane, M. E., Roenker, D. L., & Bruni, J. R. (1993). Visual attention problems as a predictor of vehicle crashes in older drivers. *Investigative Ophthalmology and Visual Science*, 34, 3110–3123.

Balota, D. A., & Chumbley, J. I. (1984). Are lexical decisions a good measure of lexical access? The role of word frequency in the neglected decision stage. *Journal of Experimental Psychology: Human Perception and Performance*, 10, 340–357.

Black, S. L. (2001). Does smelling granny relieve depressive mood? Commentary on "Rapid mood change and human odors". *Biological Psychology*, 55, 215–218.

Bower, T. G. R. (1982). *Development in infancy*. San Francisco: Freeman.

Breuer, J., & Freud, S. (1895/1955). *Studies on hysteria* (J. Strachey, trans.). London: Hogarth Press.

Briihl, D., & Inhoff, A. W. (1995). Integrating information across fixations during reading: The use of orthographic bodies and of exterior letters. *Journal of Experimental Psychology: Learning, Memory & Cognition*, 21, 55–67.

Burt, C. L. (1955). The evidence for the concept of intelligence. *British Journal of Educational Psychology*, 13, 83–98.

Burt, C. L. (1966). The genetic determination of differences in intelligence: a study of monozygotic twins reared together and apart. *British Journal of Psychology*, 57, 137–153.

Chen, D., & Haviland-Jones, J. (1999). Rapid mood change and human odours. *Physiology and Behavior*, 68, 241–250.

Chen, D. (2001). Natural human body odors can modulate mood independent of perceived odor pleasantness and intensity – a reply to Black. *Biological Psychology*, 55, 219–225.

Cohen, L. B., & Marks, K. S. (2002). How infants process addition and subtraction events. *Developmental Science*, 5, 186–212.

Cooper, M. L. (2002). Alcohol use and risky sexual behavior among college students and youth: Evaluating the evidence. *Journal of Studies on Alcohol Supplement*, 14, 101–107.

Curtis, V., Aunger, R., & Rabie, T. (2004). Evidence that disgust evolved to protect from risk of disease. *Biology Letters: Proceedings of the Royal Society of London B (Supplement)*, 271(S4), S131–S133.

Dominick, J. R. (1984). Videogames, television violence and aggression in teenagers. *Journal of Communication*, 34, 136–137.

Drachnik, C. (1994). The tongue as a graphic symbol of sexual abuse. *Art Therapy*, 11, 58–61.

Evans, D., & Norman, P. (2002). Improving pedestrian safety among adolescents: An application of the Theory of Planned Behaviour. In D. Rutter & L. Quine (eds), *Changing health behaviour: Intervention and research with social cognition models*. Buckingham: Open University Press.

Florack, U., Piontkowski, U., Rohmann, A., Balzer, T., & Perzig, S. (2003). Perceived intergroup threat and attitudes of host community members toward immigrant acculturation. *Journal of Social Psychology*, 143, 633.

Flynn, J. R. (1987). Massive IQ gains in 14 nations: What IQ tests really measure. *Psychological Bulletin*, 101, 171–191.

Fredrickson, B. L., & Levenson, R. W. (1998). Positive emotions speed recovery from the cardiovascular sequelae of negative emotions. *Cognition and Emotion*, 12, 191–220.

Galea, L. A. M., & Kimura, D. (1993). Sex differences in route learning. *Personality and Individual differences*, 14, 53–65.

Gallucci, M. (2003). I sell seashells by the seashore and my name is Jack: Comment on Pelham, Mirenberg, and Jones (2002). *Journal of Personality and Social Psychology*, 85, 789–799.

Golinkoff, R. M. (1986). "I beg your pardon?" The preverbal negotiation of failed messages. *Journal of Child Language*, 13, 455–476.

Golinkoff, R. M. (1993). When is communication a "meeting of minds"? *Journal of Child Language*, 20(1), 199–207.

Green, C. S., & Bavelier, D. (2003). Action video game modifies visual selective attention. *Nature*, 423, 534–537.

Haidt, J., McCauley, C., & Rozin, P. (1994). Individual differences in sensitivity to disgust: A scale sampling seven domains of disgust elicitors. *Personality and Individual differences*, 16, 701–713.

Herrnstein, R. J., & Murray, C. (1994). *The Bell Curve: Intelligence and Class Structure in American Life.* New York: Free Press.

Hirschfeld, L. A. (1995). Do children have a theory of race? *Cognition*, 54, 209–252.

Hirschfeld, L. A. (1996). *Race in the making*. Cambridge, MA: MIT Press.

Hirschfeld, L. A. (1997). Race, causality, and the attribution of theory-like understanding: a reply to Kim. *Cognition*, 64, 349–352.

Horn, D. B. (2001). Confounding the effects of delay and interference on memory and distortion: Commentary on Schmolck, Buffalo & Squire (2000). *Psychological Science*, 12, 180–181.

Inhoff, A. W., Radach, R., Eiter, B. M., & Skelly, M. (2003). Exterior letters are not privileged in the early stage of visual recognition during reading: Comment on Jordan, Thomas, Patching & Scott-Brown (2003). *Journal of Experimental Psychology: Learning, Memory & Cognition*, 29, 894–899.

Jacoby, R., & Glauber, N. (eds) (1995). *The Bell Curve Debate: History, Documents, Opinions*. New York: Random House.

Jones, B. T., Jones, B. C., Thomas, A. P., & Piper, J. (2003). Alcohol consumption increases attractiveness ratings of opposite-sex faces: A possible third route to risky sex. *Addiction*, 98, 1069–1075.

Jordan, T. R. (1990). Presenting words without interior letters: Superiority over single letters and influence of postmask boundaries. *Journal of Experimental Psychology: Human Perception and Performance*, 16, 893–911.

Jordan, T. R., Thomas, S. M., & Patching, G. R. (2003). Assessing the importance of letter pairs in reading – parafoveal processing is not the only view: Reply to Inhoff, Radach, Eiter & Skelly (2003). *Journal of Experimental Psychology: Learning, Memory & Cognition*, 29, 900–903.

Jordan, T. R., Thomas, S. M., Patching, G. R., & Scott-Brown, K. C. (2003). Assessing the importance of letter pairs in initial, exterior, and interior positions in reading. *Journal of Experimental Psychology: Learning, Memory & Cognition*, 29, 883–893.

Keinan, G., Barak, A., & Ramati, T. (1984). Reliablity and validity of graphological assessment in the selection process of military officers. *Perceptual and Motor Skills*, 58, 811–821.

Kim, J. J. (1997). Children's theory of race: A question of interpretation. *Cognition*, 64, 345–348.

Kimura, D. (2000). *Sex and cognition*. Cambridge, MA: MIT Press.

Kohler, W. (1925). *The mentality of apes* (E. Winter, trans.). London: Kegan Paul, Trench, Trubner & Co., Ltd.

Lieven, E. M. (1978). Conversations between mothers and children: Individual differences and their precise implications for the study of language learning. In N. Waterson & C. Snow (eds), *Social and pragmatic factors in language acquisition* (pp. 173–187). New York: John Wiley.

Ligout, S., & Porter, R. H. (2003). Social discrimination in lambs: the role of indirect familiarization and methods of assessment. *Animal Behaviour*, 65, 1109–1115.

Loftus, E. F., & Palmer, J. C. (1974). Reconstruction of automobile destruction. *Journal of Verbal Learning and Verbal Behaviour*, 13, 585–589.

Lilienfeld, S. O., Wood, J. M., & Garb, H. N. (2000). The scientific status of projective techniques. *Psychological Science in the Public Interest*, 1, 27–66.

Marriott, T., Reilly, T., & Miles (1993). The effect of physiological stress on cognitive performance in a simulation of soccer. In T. Reilly & J. Clarys & A. Stibbe (eds), *Science and football II* (pp. 261–264). London: E. and F.N. Spon.

Martin, C., Vu, H., Kellas, G., & Metcalf, K. (1999). Strength of discourse context as a determinant of the subordinate bias effect. *Quarterly Journal of Experimental Psychology*, 52A, 813–839.

Martin, L. (1986). Eskimo words for snow: A case study in the genesis and decay of an anthropological example. *American Anthropologist*, 88, 418–423.

Mascerehas, D. R. D., Collins, D., & Mortimer, P. (2002). The art of reason versus the exactness of science in elite refereeing. Comments on Plessner and Betch (2001). *Journal of Sport & Exercise Psychology*, 24, 328–333.

Mayer, R. E., Tajika, H., & Stanley, C. (1991). Mathematical problem solving in Japan and the United States: A controlled comparison. *Journal of Educational Psychology*, 83, 69–72.

McLeod, J., Atkin, C., & Chaffee, S. (1972). Adolescents, parents and television use. In G. A. Comstock and E. A. Rubenstein (eds), *Television and Social Behaviour (vol. 3), Television and Adolescent Aggressiveness.* Washington, DC: Government Printing Office.

Medin, D. L., & Shoben, E. J. (1988). Context and structure in conceptual combination. *Cognitive Psychology*, 20, 158–190.

Mervis, C. B., & Klein-Tasman, B. P. (2004). Methodological issues in matching group designs: alpha levels for control variable comparisons and measurement characteristics of control and target variables. *Journal of Autism and Developmental Disorders*, 34, 7–17.

Miller, T., Velleman, R., Rigby, K., Orford, J., Tod, A., Copello, A., & Bennett, G. (1997). The use of vignettes in the analysis of interview data: Relatives of people with drug problems. In N. Hayes (ed.), *Doing qualitative analysis in psychology* (pp. 201–225). Hove: Psychology Press.

Monsell, S., Doyle, M. C., & Haggard, P. N. (1989). Effects of frequency on visual word recognition tasks: Where are they? *Journal of Experimental Psychology: General*, 118, 43–71.

Neisser, U. (ed.). (1998). *The rising curve.* Washington: American Psychological Association.

Neter, E., & Ben-Shakhar, G. (1989). The predictive validity of graphological inferences: A meta-analytic approach. *Personality and Individual Differences*, 10, 737–745.

Pelham, B. W., Mirenberg, M. C., & Jones, J. T. (2002). Why Susie sells seashells by the seashore: Implicit egotism and major life decisions. *Journal of Personality and Social Psychology*, 82, 469–487.

Plessner, H., & Betch (2001). Sequential effects in important referee decisions. The case of penalties in soccer. *Journal of Sport & Exercise Psychology*, 23, 254–259.

Piaget, J. (1954). *The construction of reality in the child.* New York: Basic Books.

Rabbitt, P., & Abson, V. (1990). Lost and found: some logical and methodological limitations to self-report questionnaires as tools to study cognitive aging. *British Journal of Psychology*, 81, 1–16.

Rayner, K., Binder, K. S., & Duffy, S. A. (1999). Contextual strength and the subordinate bias effect: Comment on Martin, Vu, Kellas, and Metcalf. *The Quarterly Journal of Experimental*, 52A, 841–852.

Reynolds, D., Nicolson, R. I., & Hambly, H. (2003). Evaluation of an exercise-based treatment for children with reading difficulties. *Dyslexia: An International Journal of Research and Practice*, 9(1), 48–71.

Rozin, P., Haidt, J., McCauley, C., Dunlop, L., & Ashmore, M. (1999). Individual differences in disgust sensitivity: Comparisons and evaluations of paper-and-pencil versus behavioral measures. *Journal of Research in Personality*, 33, 330–351.

Sawchuck, C. N., Lohr, J. M., Tolin, D. F., Lee, T. C., & Kleinknecht, R. A. (2000). Disgust sensitivity and contamination fears in spider and blood-injection-injury phobias. *Behaviour Research and Therapy*, 38, 753–762.

Schmolck, H., Buffalo, E. A., & Squire, L. R. (2000). Memory distortions develop over time: Recollections of the O. J. Simpson trial verdict after 15 and 30 months. *Psychological Science*, 11, 39–45.

Schwartz, G. E. R., Russek, L. G. S., Nelson, L. A., & Barentsen, C. (2001). Accuracy and replicability of anomolous after-death communication across highly skilled mediums. *Journal of the Society for Psychical Research*, 65, 1–25.

Seidenberg, M. S., Tanenhaus, M. K., Leiman, J. M., & Bienkowski, M. (1982). Automatic access of the meanings of ambiguous words in context: Some limitations of knowledge-based processing. *Cognitive Psychology*, 14, 489–537.

Shatz, M., & O'Reilly, A. (1990). Conversational or communicative skill? A reassessment of two-year-olds' behaviour in miscommunication episodes. *Journal of Child Language*, 17, 131–146.

Shaughnessy, J. J., Zechmeister, E. B., & Zechmeister, J. S. (2003). *Research methods in psychology* (6th edn). New York: McGraw-Hill.

Shwe, H. I., & Markman, E. M. (2001). Young children's appreciation of the mental impact of communicative signals. In M. Tomasello & E. Bates (eds), *Language development: Essential readings* (pp. 62–75). Oxford: Blackwell.

Smith, E. E., Osherson, D. N., Rips, L. J., & Keane, M. (1988). Combining prototypes: A selective modification model. *Cognitive Science*, 12, 485–528.

Snyder, J., & Rogers, K. (2002). The violent adolescent: The urge to destroy versus the urge to feel alive. *The American Journal of Psychoanalysis*, 62, 237–253.

Spitzer, R. (2003). Can some gay men and lesbians change their sexual orientation? 200 participants reporting a change from homosexual to heterosexual orientation. *Archives of Sexual Behavior*, 32, 403–417.

Stigler, J. W., & Miller, K. F. (1993). A good match is hard to find: Comment on Mayer, Tajika, and Stanley (1991). *Journal of Educational Psychology*, 85, 554–559.

Swinney, D. A. (1979). Lexical access during sentence comprehension: (Re)Consideration of context effects. *Journal of Verbal Learning and Verbal Behaviour*, 18, 645–659.

Tabachnik, B. G., & Fidell, L. S. (2001). *Using multivariate statistics* (4th edn). Needham Heights, MA: Allyn & Bacon.

Taft, M. (1992). The body of BOSS: Subsyllabic units in the lexical processing of polysyllabic words. *Journal of Experimental Psychology: Human Perception and Performance*, 18, 1004–1014.

Tenney, Y. (1984). Ageing and the misplacing of objects. *British Journal of Developmental Psychology*, 2, 43–50.

Tourangeau, R., Rips, L. J., & Rasinski, K. (2000). *The psychology of survey response*. Cambridge: Cambridge University Press.

Trimpop, R., & Kirkcaldy, B. (1997). Personality predictors of driving accidents. *Personality and Individual Differences*, 23, 147–152.

Watson, D. G., & Humphreys, G. W. (1997). Visual marking. Prioritizing selection for new objects by top-down attentional inhibition of old objects. *Psychological Review*, 104(1), 90–122.

Wynn, K. (1992). Addition and subtraction by human infants. *Nature*, 358, 749–750.

INDEX